Pie Corbett
Brian Moses

My Grandma's motorbike

Story Writing in the Primary School

Cool Granny

Oxford U

Oxford University Press, Walton Street, Oxford OX2 6DP

Oxford   New York   Toronto
Delhi   Bombay   Calcutta   Madras   Karachi
Petaling Jaya   Singapore   Hong Kong   Tokyo
Nairobi   Dar es Salaam   Cape Town
Melbourne   Auckland

and associated companies in
Berlin   Ibadan

Oxford is a trade mark of Oxford University Press

ISBN 019 918291 4

Typeset by MS Filmsetting Limited, Frome, Somerset
Printed in Great Britain by Biddles Ltd., Guildford.

Cover illustration by Rachel McLaren, Cuxton County Junior School, Kent

Contents

In memory of my father who read, told and listened. P.C.

About the authors

Pie Corbett was Headteacher of a primary school and is now Senior Lecturer in Primary Education at the Cheltenham and Gloucester College of Higher Education. He has run writing workshops in many schools and held various residencies. His poetry has appeared in many anthologies and in 1989 *The Kingfisher Playtime Treasury*, the first major collection for children of playground rhymes and games, was published.

Brian Moses is a professional writer. Previously he taught, for thirteen years, in East Sussex primary schools. He now visits schools on a regular basis running workshops with children, talking to teachers and performing his own poetry, much of which has been included in various anthologies. A collection of his poetry, *Leave Your Teddy Behind*, was published in 1988. Brian Moses is editor of *Bookquest*, a termly review of children's books.

Pie Corbett and Brian Moses are co-authors of *Catapults and Kingfishers – Teaching Poetry in Primary Schools* (Oxford University Press 1986), and *Poetry for Projects* (Scholastic Publications 1989).

Introduction

Why stories?

Tell me
a story
about a
ghost that
shrieks and
groans, a skeleton
that rattles, a
monster huge and
crawly, a beast
so wild and fierce.
Tell me a story about
a cat which is spotty
and cross, a cat which
sits on the witches
broom, a cat that can fly up
to the moon near to the
bright stars.

Katie Sillcock, 7 yrs.

It was breakfast time and Poppy suddenly turned to me and said, 'Stop pestering me and go to your workhouse.' Coming from a two year-old, I felt this was a bit strong. It was only later when I was reading *Postman Pat's Safari* by John Cunliffe that I came across the place where she had learned that phrase:

'Every morning, Katy and Tom Pottage asked their mother, "Is it time for the trip, yet?"
And every morning, Mrs Pottage said, "Not yet. It won't be long. Now stop pestering me, and get off to school." '

Stories are magical. Anyone who has shared a story with a child knows that. Some stories we can take and leave, but others echo in the mind. I wonder which stories you remember from your childhood?

When children come to school they expect to learn how to read and write. Every day thousands of children sit down to 'write a story'. If we took every page from every story written by school children in one week, and put them edge to edge, we could circle the Earth – several times, I guess. And yet, despite spending so much time churning out stories, many children still end up struggling to find anything they feel is worth writing. For them, there seems to be little magic in writing their own stories. Worse still, we have all taught children who when asked to write a story look blank and say, 'I can't write'. What they usually mean is that they cannot spell accurately or that their handwriting is very poorly formed. Because everyone can tell stories. We spend most of our talking time telling stories. And, indeed, those who find writing difficult may be those who can tell stories the most powerfully. Follow them into the playground and listen.

We tell stories about all kinds of things: about what happened last night when Dad tripped over the cat; about the plumber being called out; about what we saw on the TV; about Nan taking us blackberry picking; about seeing the polar bear in London zoo pacing up and down, and going back the next year and finding that he's still pacing up and down; about our sister's first tooth; about our family histories. We tell stories that are funny, frightening, or sad. We spend a lot of our time re-creating for others what has happened to us; we take moments of significance and re-create them through telling. And the more the experience meant to us, the more we need to talk about it.

A crude example of this would be that when my father died, my mother went over the details of the car accident again and again. She needed to. She needed to try and use the story of what happened to understand the inexplicable. She needed to communicate how she felt to us, so that we could share in the experience. And it seemed after a very long time that she no longer needed to tell us that story. She stopped seeing the crashed car every time she closed her eyes. It was as if telling her story had helped her distance herself from what had happened. It now held the distance of a crafted tale.

A similar sort of example is to do with my younger brother, Hereward. When my great-aunt died of cancer he rushed upstairs to his bedroom. He was only eight and had been very close to her. None of us felt like following him and we let him be. Half an hour later he came downstairs with a piece of paper.

He had written about it.

'There was trouble in heaven. God needed a right-hand man. He looked around and there was no one. But he saw Mabel Elizabeth Violet Gay and so on the 26th April 1975 at 2.30 pm he took her up into Heaven to help him.'

You can imagine the silence as we read what he had written. No one quite knew what to say. He did. 'I'm going out to play on my bike,' he shouted, racing outside with a laugh. Quite simply, the inexplicable had happened. He made a story of it, shared it and had begun to come to terms with it. I have told you these two stories because stories help us understand things much better than being told. A story is an experience through which we might learn about ourselves and the world.

These, of course, are great and traumatic moments. Most of our story-telling concerns the everyday moments. It grows out of conversations, snippets, playground jokes, gossip, speculation, new things that have happened, things we're worried about, stories passed on about other people, stories gleaned from TV and our reading ... and we are all doing it, very busily, for a large part of our talking lives.

There is more to it than that. Interwoven into telling about our lives and listening to others telling about their lives come the stories that are written in books, read on the radio, seen on TV, told in the community, repeated family stories and tales told on the knee. These are stories that have been shaped for telling. They are more carefully crafted than our anecdotal tales.

As children become story-makers they blend their own lives with what they learn about stories from written tales. Initially, they may borrow words or phrases – as Poppy did in the earlier example. They soon become aware that creating a 'story' may have some differences from talking about our own lives. There are different ways of starting a story – 'Once upon a time / One day...' Things happen in stories. You can make things up in a story. Stories are about what happens and how everything is all right in the end. One morning Poppy stood at the edge of our bed and with the intent look of a story-maker slowly said,

'Daisy Dumpit. I put him on the line to dry outside. I went inside cos

I was feeling a little bit cold and I called, "Mummy, Mummy".'

Without knowing it we are all story-tellers. We use stories to learn about ourselves and our world, to explain to others what our experience is like. We make sense of what happens by telling, by sharing, by listening and by responding to stories. To develop as story-makers we take our own life stories and interlace them with what we learn from crafted tales. What does this all mean for the teacher with a class of thirty-five seven-year-olds, working in a hut on a wet Thursday afternoon?

In finding out we need to consider the following:

- Helping children develop as story-tellers;
- Sharing a response to story-books;
- Children as authors.

Helping children develop as story-tellers

What do you need for a story-telling session? A story to tell, someone to tell it, and someone to listen.

Creating the climate

It is important to set the right atmosphere. Firstly, if children are to tell stories they need good listeners. There is nothing more off-putting than beginning to talk about something and finding that no one is listening. The teacher has to become a good listener and should act as a model for the children: 'Quiet please, I'm interested in what Sarah is saying.' Get the class to establish their own rules for story-telling time:

To enjoy story-telling time we have to:

- be quiet,
- not move round,
- listen carefully,
- be ready to enjoy the tale ...

Stories can be told in pairs, in small groups or to the whole class – after each session the tellers and listeners can reflect on how well it went. Did people listen, did someone spoil it, how did Sarah make it exciting, which was your favourite bit ...? The business of becoming good at listening is important because it helps to give the teller confidence. If the teller gets stuck, the right questioning can help to prompt the next part of the story – 'What happened next?' 'Tell us more about that.' 'What did you do then?' The exciting thing about telling stories is that the story can change with the mood of the audience. In this way, story-telling differs from a storybook.

But what should the story be about? You need to find a story that interests you, that you feel involved in, that you have a clear picture of as it proceeds and that you really want to tell. For starters you need look no further than your own anecdotes. The roots of story-telling lie in the infant class news/sharing sessions. Here you learn the importance of talking clearly, of looking at your audience, of talking slowly enough and not racing, of translating a series of events into words and of what is worth telling and what might not be. A good story has significance. Why do we listen to a good story? Because we want to find out what happens. A good story has a dilemma and we listen to find out how it will be resolved. This element is missing from so many children's written stories which end up as a series of events in which there is no conflict. To overcome this, children need to become genuine story-tellers – telling the tale before writing it down.

Story games and starting points

- In a circle. Someone starts to tell a story. Everyone tells a sentence in turn and the story moves round the circle.
- In a circle. The story moves round as above but you are not allowed to use the words 'and' or 'the'. If you do, miss a turn.
- Tell the class a story. In groups, they have to retell the tale.
- Retell a story in the round. If someone can't think of what happened next they miss a turn.
- Read or tell a story about something that happened to you when you were younger – encourage an exchange of anecdotes.
- In a group work out a story and each take turns in the telling.
- Practise story-telling in pairs before sharing with the group. Get your partner to tell you how your telling went. You could

jot down the main scenes.

- Tell a story using pictures or objects to help.
- Tape your story. Listen to it carefully. See if you can retell it better.
- Send your taped stories to a class in another school.
- Tell a story that starts with a warning, for example, ' "Don't go near that box," said Mum.' In pairs decide what might happen and how it will come all right. Practise telling the story and try it out in a larger group.
- Prepare a story to tell to someone in another class or to a younger child.
- Make a tape recording of a regular storytime each week, for a younger class to listen to. (A bit like 'Listen with Mother' – you could begin this project by listening to some radio stories.)
- Spread a story throughout the school.
- Tell a story and see if the class can guess if it is true or false.
- Tell a story with one false part in it. The class have to guess which bit is not true. This game can be played in teams.
- Tell a story based on truth, but which you have elaborated.
- Tell a story to explain a natural phenomenon such as why the sun rises, what makes thunder, etc.
- Tell another story about a story character.
- Retell a story you've heard from someone else's viewpoint.
- Go home and ask your family to tell you their favourite story. Retell it in school. Find out about your parents'/grandparents' early lives. Retell any interesting incidents.
- Invite in people from the local community with stories to tell.
- Play 'Fortunately/unfortunately'. Set the scene for a story. Each person takes it in turn. The first teller has to turn the story in a positive direction – 'Tom woke up and the sun shone brightly. He jumped out of bed.' The next person has to turn it in a negative direction – 'In the distance thunder rumbled. He was so surprised that he tripped over and banged his head.'
- The old king is dying. He can only be saved by a funny story. Everyone tells a funny story. The story-teller who gets the biggest laugh is made king's adviser.

- Read stories with patterns and repetition. In pairs construct a tale that has a repeating line.
- Make up a story using puppets, models or farm animals etc.
- Very young children need stories with happy endings. Older children might tell a story with a sad ending.
- Tell a story in which the main character is a girl.
- Bring in a photograph or a treasured object from home. Tell why it is important.
- Form regular story groups which help the participants create stories, listen to and comment on each other's stories.
- Invite in a professional story-teller.
- Listen to stories in another language. Guess what each story was about. What sort of story did it sound like?
- Invent a school story. Take photos of the main scenes. Tell the story that goes with the photos.
- Tell a story that starts with 'Supposing you could . . .', or 'What would happen if . . .', or 'Last night I saw . . .', or 'This is about a time I was really afraid/happy/sad/angry/in trouble/told a lie . . .'
- Have a swap-a-story day. See who can collect the most new stories in one day.
- Hold a story-telling festival. Invite in parents, people from the community, and professional tellers. Erect story-stands and story-booths, which class members can visit and hear each others' stories.
- Tell a well-known story but change its ending or characters.
- Tell half a story to a partner. Your partner has to finish the story for you. Then swap over.

Guidelines for story-tellers

Story-tellers need time. They need time to practise, to think their ideas through and to try their tale out. At first don't expect anything very long. Length and depth come with confidence. Use plenty of praise to encourage. Small story-telling groups and pairs provide a more inviting setting for those who lack confidence. The following process may help:

1 Decide what the story is going to be about. The plot is vital.

2 Decide how you are going to tell the story – is it happening now, or has it already happened? Are you going to be in the story ('I woke up') or will it be about someone else ('She woke up')?

3 Work out the details. Draw or jot down the main parts of the story. Flow charts of the sequence of action can be useful.

4 Try out the story on your partner, on your group, or into a tape recorder. Get some reactions to help you improve. Sometimes it helps if someone else in the group retells your story, adding to it.

5 Practise a few times. Go over the story, saying it in your head.

6 When you are ready, tell your story. Don't be afraid to change it as you go along if something new occurs to you.

Avoid stories which are reports. 'We heard a noise, I got out of bed, I went downstairs, I saw a burglar, I caught him', reports what happened, but it isn't a story. To move into a story, try telling what happened by placing yourself in the action. 'I sat up in bed and listened. I could hear the sound of something scratching at the downstairs window...'

There are dangers in trying to 'learn' a story. The children are desperately trying to remember which words come next and consequently can dry up completely. Each time they tell a story, it can come alive anew. Each time it may be slightly different. From anecdotes, children soon move into elaborating, inventing, adapting and retelling. The constraints of handwriting and spelling are removed and they can compose at greater length and with more relish. Above all, through telling stories children can come to see the point of writing them down – they are preserved for others. Oral story-telling prepares the ground for and enriches their written stories.

A classroom of story-tellers who create and share together becomes a community within which children can use stories to represent, shape and communicate experiences in their own lives. Hidden fears can be relished in safe delight. We can visit new worlds and take a step out of ourselves.

The teacher as story-teller can weave the magic and mystery of myths, legends and fairy-tales from throughout the world, emphasising the reassuring pattern of good triumphing over evil. Before I tell a story I like to rehearse it myself – I usually tell the story aloud, often while I am travelling in the car. I aim for an inviting beginning that gets straight into the action. You don't need too many characters, or the plot can become confusing. Of course, you need a problem that creeps in early on, plenty of fast-moving action and an end that satisfies. I like to try to find an end that also surprises, by not being too obvious – a twist in the tale. One final tip: it is useful with younger children to have a rhyme or repetitive phrase that they can join in with – or questions that they can call out the answers to.

If you are nervous without the security of a book to read from, I can only say I sympathise. All you can do is have a go – and remember you get better at it the more you do it. Fix on one story. Prepare it carefully – then see if you can try it out on a number of classes over a period of several weeks. You will certainly find it easier as you go along.

Sharing a response to story-books

From the very start of school, children will be sharing story-books in the classroom. It is through sharing stories that children come to understand and develop their own use of story structures – beginnings, endings, settings, developing characters, a series of events that flow from each other, a logical sequence, resolving a conflict. This understanding is woven into their developing ability to talk reflectively about their own lives. We see the development of an ability to adopt, adapt, retell and invent stories.

When we listen to stories told or read to us, we re-create the story within our own minds. It is not a passive activity. And it is most likely that within a class no one creates quite the same story – the setting looks different, that characters are not quite the same – for we take experiences from our own lives and bring them to the story. It follows that each time we encounter a story we've already heard before, the experience will be slightly different.

14

In the 'ideas' sections of this book we suggest that children should have the opportunity to develop an in-depth, creative, active involvement in responding to stories. This response will take them into the world of the story in order to discover what the story means for them and what it means to others. In doing so they may discover more about themselves and more about the worlds that others inhabit. Most of our suggestions for ways into stories come in the form of group activities. These provide a chance to discover other people's responses and viewpoints as well as a chance to talk our way towards an understanding for ourselves. This is not possible by whole class teaching, as fewer children will be able to participate and respond. When planning activities we need to consider whether the activities will help the children understand the story better.

We suggest that two sorts of activities might arise from using a story as a starting point for deepening understanding.

a Some activities might help us understand the story better, by exploring the themes, characters, settings and events.

b Some activities might be of a cross-curricular nature and lead into learning about things related to the story, but not necessarily those which will help us find out for ourselves what the story might be about. For example, talking about life-saving while reading *The Night Swimmers* by Betsy Byars.

When developing responses to stories it may be useful to consider what happens before, during and after we have read.

Before reading the whole story

- Read the class the first chapter. Guess the title.
- Look at the cover. Guess the title.
- Tell the class the title – in groups decide what the story might be about.
- Jot down initial thoughts, impressions, ideas, feelings.
- Jot down and discuss any experiences you have had that this story reminds you of.
- Do you think you will like/dislike this story? Why?
- What do you think is going to happen next? Decide in groups and report back.

During the story

- Use puppets and models to act out part of the story or to set out a scene from the story.
- Retell the story so far.
- What is this character thinking? Draw a cartoon and fill in a speech bubble to show what a character is thinking.
- Write headlines based on what happens in the story for the local papers.
- Pretend you are a local TV crew reporting on a scene in the story. Send a news bulletin describing what is happening.
- Interview a character from the story – as if you were a radio or TV reporter, a journalist or a police officer.
- Set out your favourite scene, using Plasticine on a polythene sheet.
- Take a character who has just left the story. Discuss what he/she might be doing and report back.
- Write the next chapter.
- Stop the story at a crucial point and get groups to role-play the rest of the scene. Then see what happens in the story.
- When a character is in a dilemma, ask pairs to decide what they would do.
- As the tale unfolds, discuss what you think the story is about. Try to move from retelling the tale to deciding what the themes are.
- List questions you'd like to ask the main character/author/illustrator.
- What do you think is the most important question we need to know the answer to? Discuss and report back, giving reasons for your answers.
- Suggest a different style and say why you chose it.
- Draw your favourite character.
- Write a character's diary for a day in the story.
- Write a letter from one character who has left the story to someone still in the action.
- Find someone who doesn't know the story. Tell them what has happened so far. Practise before doing this.

- Retell the story as if you were one of the characters. Let other members of the group question you.
- To keep track of the story, develop a flow chart showing the main scenes in the right sequence. Add to it as the story moves along.
- Design a WANTED poster for the villain.
- Draw a picture of each character. Choose your favourites and list their likes/dislikes.
- Close your eyes. Which is your favourite bit from the story? Draw it or write about why that piece means something to you.
- At the start of a chapter read the first few lines. What do you think is going to happen? Why do you think this? Give reasons, backed up by clues from what you have already read.
- Draw a family tree showing who is related to whom.
- Draw a map of the story showing where main events have occurred.
- Draw the main character's bedroom.
- Describe what has happened from a particular character's viewpoint.
- Make a collection of objects, pictures and documents that are mentioned in the story.
- Advertise something important from the story (for example, Bilbo's ring in *The Hobbit*).
- In pairs pretend to be two of the characters from the book. You have met up, and you are fed up with what is going on. Tell each other how you feel and what you think you should do.
- Paint, print, draw or describe a setting from the story. Write a travel brochure for the place where the story is located.
- Who do you think is right? Describe different characters' points of view and decide which is right.
- Predict in groups what will happen next, but choose to make it a sad, happy or angry event.
- Look at estate agents' sales leaflets. Design a leaflet for a house in the story (for example, Bilbo's hobbit hole).

- Write an end-of-term report for the villain or heroine.
- Make a passport for one of the characters you liked.
- Which character is most like you? Why do you think so?

After the story

- Jot down what you are feeling immediately after the story ends.
- Discuss the ending. Was it satisfactory? Decide on a different ending. Share these and discuss them.
- Design a new jacket cover, complete with author's blurb.
- Design an advert to sell this story to others.
- Design an appropriate review sheet (for example, a dragon-shaped sheet for *The Hobbit*) with a rating of 1 to 10 for how much you liked it. Write a review of the story for others to read.
- Would you lend this story to your best friend/worst enemy and why?
- Has anything changed during the story, such as people or places? What has changed and how did it happen? Are things better, or worse? Why do you think this?
- Look back for clues in the story that could have told you what was going to happen.
- Does anything still puzzle you about this story? Share your puzzles, listen, suggest, try to unravel, ask each other questions.
- Play the 'Statements Game'. Write or collect a number of statements about the story. Either:

a Give each group a copy of the same ten statements. They have to put them into an order, with the one they agree with most at the top. The statements are then glued on to a piece of paper and pinned on the wall. Compare each group's list.

b Give groups a collection of twenty to thirty statements. Let them put them into one of three categories – those they agree with, those they are not too sure about and those they disagree with completely.

- Design a card or board game to go with the story (for example, a bicycle race game to accompany *The Mustang Machine*).
- Were you surprised by what happened at the end of the book? Look back at your initial impressions and ideas. Have your ideas changed? What do you think now?
- Did you change what you felt about any of the characters?
- What was your most memorable scene? Describe it as if you were a bystander.
- Pretend you are one of the characters and write what you feel about what you are doing now.
- Write a sequel.
- In your group illustrate the main scenes from the story. Decide which scenes are most important. Make a presentation, talking about your choice.
- Would you place this in your 'Desert Island Story' list? Why/ why not?
- Write a letter to the author or illustrator. What would you like to find out?
- Retell the story as a cartoon.
- It is six months after the end of the story. Pretend you are a character from the story. Retell your part in the story and include what has happened since.
- Provide a long list of characteristics – let groups choose the five words that they feel best describe the villain/heroine.
- Represent scenes through model-making. Use collage to depict the main themes. Set the ending of the story to music.

Looking more closely at the text

Some activities to encourage children to look more closely at the text.

- Prediction. Cut up the story into parts. Give the group part of the story. What do they think will happen next? Then give them the next part of the story. Again they have to read and suggest what might happen next. Encourage them to search for clues in their reading and reflect on what they already know about the characters, before making their suggestions.

This is rather like the sports quiz on TV where contestants are shown a sporting event for a few seconds before the action freezes. They have to say what they think happened next.

- Cloze procedure. Give out a copy of the text with selected words or phrases omitted. Groups discuss what they consider would be the most appropriate words to put in.

- Copy out part of the text but change some of the words. Groups have to underline where they think the text has been changed, and suggest what a better version might be.

- Sequencing. This can be done with pictures from a story-book, simple texts, cartoons and more complex stories. Cut up the text and give it to the group in an envelope. Can they sort it into the right order?

- Underline key words and phrases. Circle clues in the text that give an indication of what is going to happen. Put an asterisk by passages that tell us something about a character.

The above ideas are best carried out as group activities to give the opportunity for the exchange of opinions and ideas – the chance to engage with others' thinking, and learn from them. Groups should report back to the class or teacher so that differences in viewpoints and understandings can be explored.

Organising groups

It may well be that your class are not used to working on group activities. They may have been 'grouped' but never had to talk their way co-operatively through a task in search of understanding. The chances are that they will take some time to develop useful group behaviour, but persistence on your part and helping them establish their own ground rules will help. Here are some suggestions to consider when organising group work:

a Give clear instructions and ask someone to repeat what they have to do, to check they've understood. Remind them to listen at this point – or you will end up repeating yourself. Possibly hand out written instructions. Make the task one that challenges and encourages group interaction.

b Encourage groups to select a note-taker/someone to report back, and a chairperson if appropriate.

c Set a time limit – initially make it quite brief, say 10 minutes. Extend this as they become better at it.

d Expect more noise – but don't tolerate shouting, etc.

e Move round from group to group. Make sure that they are working on the task. Bring them back to the task and to the story – listen, praise, encourage, ask open questions to lead their thinking on, make suggestions to open up unexplored avenues, but don't tell them the answer. Teachers find it very tempting to have a preconceived idea of what children should say. If you leap in with your viewpoint, you rob them of the chance of coming to their own understanding. Your most powerful teaching tools will be to become a good listener and a good questioner.

f Sometimes leave groups alone.

g Hold a reporting-back session. Let each group make their presentation. Also encourage groups to talk about how they worked as a group – what was useful and what was not. Edge them towards establishing their own ground rules. If groups are not to report back publicly, ask for a written report, a statement, a list of suggestions, etc.

h Sometimes put a group in a quiet place and tape-record a short session. Get the group to listen to their talk afterwards and encourage them to identify good group behaviour – for example, not dominating, taking turns, listening, building on what someone else has said, encouraging comments, asking questions, keeping on task, reminding the group of the task, praise for comments, making new suggestions, dropping an idea when the others don't agree, bringing in someone who has been quiet.

The reading journal

This could be a personal notebook, a folder, a scrapbook, or an exercise book. In it are collected thoughts, ideas, impressions and comments on books read, with the dates when they were read. The journal acts as a source of information about what has been read and the reader's personal response. Encourage children to respond before, during and after reading. This is a notebook, a learning arena, and as such should perhaps not be looked at with a view to checking on formal presentation, but rather to make a response to the content. The teacher could write in her own reactions, thoughts, ideas for further reading, anecdotes, etc.

When an extended project focusing on a story is being carried out, a book about the book could be made, with the various responses, drawings, maps, diagrams, flow-charts, letters, etc included.

Where, when, what?

If we are hoping children will catch a love of stories, the conditions for reading them should be as good as we can possibly make them.

If we think that stories are important, why are they so often relegated to the curriculum fourth-division place, at 3.15 p.m. every afternoon? To calm the children down before their mums get hold of them? This leaves no chance for response in an active way. Be bold – start the day the story way . . .

Almost every child I have asked dislikes reading in school and is happiest reading at home in bed. The ideal place to read is somewhere comfortable, where you are relaxed. A place where you will not be disturbed by dinner ladies with messages. A place where the children can see you and you can see them. It's a great shame that the idea of a carpeted story-corner dies out in most junior classrooms.

Younger children may share stories with Big Books, so they can see the text and pictures, or in smaller groups where the teacher has developed the fine art of showing the pictures and reading the text upside-down. Groups might all have a copy of a story to share and discuss. Pairs might read together.

What should we read? Quite simply we need to provide a variety of the best. All children must have access to good literature. Stories and poems from the world family that will interest, excite, engage and meet the needs of our children. Stories we enjoy, so that we can impart some of our own excitement. Stories that matter to us as a community. Stories from our community. Stories written by adults and children. The stories should be sometimes simple, sometimes just beyond our understanding, stories that we might not have encountered, stories that challenge. The stories need to invite us to engage with them, and there is no shortage! Stories should sometimes be recommended by children and read aloud by those confident enough.

The responses we give will focus on what we enjoyed ('I liked the bit where ...') on what we're unsure about ('I don't see why ...') and through the discussion our understanding grows. We look for patterns in what happens, in the plot, the characters, the language and our responses ('Yes, I felt that too', 'That's interesting, you may be right', 'Yes, I hadn't thought of that'.)

The classroom can become a place where story worlds are encountered. All children should also have access to the full range of literature; they should be able to take home stories to savour alone, stories to share and stories to have read to them.

Children as authors

Stories are a natural means of celebrating and coping with our experience.

I used to think that children learn to write by writing. It is important to have a go. After all, you learn how to ride a bike by having a go – not by reading the manual. I still believe it to be true; but I also think there is more to it than that.

a Children learn to write by writing. They need the chance to become authors and work towards producing stories in similar ways to an author.

b Children learn about writing by seeing others write and being involved with other people writing. They learn by imitating, by getting the feel of how it's done, by reflecting on how someone else approaches the task.

c They learn to write by working alongside someone who can already write. They need to have demonstrations of how writing is done, and have someone to help them reflect on what they are doing and how best to approach the task.

d Children learn to write stories by telling, reading and hearing them. They learn about the nature of a story and pick up

23

structures from hearing and reading stories. The more actively engaged they are when they respond to stories, the better. As they write, they listen to the story-teller in their heads.

A story-writing workshop

Let's imagine that your class are active story-tellers. They thrive on the stories they read and that you read with them. The conditions are ripe for story-writing and making that leap into becoming authors.

Getting started

Sometimes you will suggest an idea, sometimes the story will already have been told several times, sometimes the children will have a story they want to tell. Some story-writers like to start and see where the tale takes them. Others like to plan beforehand. Children need to discover which approaches work well for them. The problem with launching straight in may be that the child focuses too much on the plot and the story becomes a series of actions joined by 'and then'. If this occurs, slow them down. Suggest they plan each scene ahead. Give plenty of time to the story, so that it can take several weeks and does not have to be finished in a forty-minute dash. Let them tell before they write.

The problem with planning ahead may be that some of the excitement of writing the story is taken away. After all, you already know what is going to happen. Some authors like to write in order to find out what is going to happen – Alistair MacLean said that whenever he couldn't find a good story to read he sat down and wrote one. What often happens with planning ahead is that even though you feel you have the perfect plot, when you come to write the story you find that other things creep in. Characters don't behave as expected, and you have to change the plan anyway. Some useful planning techniques are:

Brainstorming – Write very quickly any ideas that spring to mind, not bothering to sift them until you have quite a long list. For instance, you could use this idea to help find a title. Ask the children to list as many titles as they can think of that they would like to write about. Give them one minute. When the minute is up, ask them to underline their favourite three and then discuss with a partner to try and decide which might be best to use. Brainstorming could also be used for jotting down ideas for the plot, things that could happen, to describe a place or character.

Taping – Tape-record the story before writing.

Making pictures – Close your eyes and try to see the place, event or character you are writing about. Try to watch the action like a film in your mind. What happens next?

Diagrams – Use a flow-chart of boxes and write in each box what happens next. Then when writing, take each box as the next section and spend time elaborating the action. Use a spider web to jot down ideas. Use a column to list suggestions. Draw the story box by box, like a cartoon.

Story-group/partner – Tell your story idea to your group or partner before you begin. Ask for suggestions as to how it might be developed. Retell it to another group.

During these planning sessions the teacher needs to be moving round, listening, suggesting, asking questions and encouraging children to explain what their ideas are.

Getting the writing done

When children settle down to write there are two concerns.

a What am I going to say? (Composing)

b How do I get that down on paper? (Transcribing – spelling, handwriting and presentation)

Most children have plenty to say but many find they have problems with spelling and handwriting. It is inappropriate at this stage to expect accurate spelling and immaculate presentation. This is the early drafting stage. The focus should be upon the quality of the story, listening, following and capturing the story-teller in our heads.

Tell the children to invent their spellings, or act as a scribe for them. This can be done with individuals or in a group. Many teachers of early writers like to scribe on a board in front of the group so they can see the process in action. This is the writing equivalent of sharing a Big Book. Parents or other children, as well as the teacher, might act as a scribe. This leaves the child free to compose. As the children write, move round the room, praising, supporting and showing interest. If someone is stuck ask a question to lead the story on, for example 'Tell me what happened next'. Or make several suggestions. Or ask a question like 'What would happen if ...?' If the story is going nowhere and doesn't seem to have anything happening in it at all, ask a question that might suggest a problem, such as 'What's that lion going to do to the little boy?'

Writing can be a solitary activity or carried out in groups. The group can plan together, and divide up chapters to be written, illustrations and bookmaking tasks. Time and regular reporting-back sessions are required.

It is useful to watch how different children tackle their writing. Some write very quickly, others work in short bursts, some seem slow. Watch to see if they are seated comfortably at a good height, in good lighting, that the pencil grip is not too tight, the room not too stuffy, there are no distractions to stop the flow. As they write move round and begin to engage in helping them to take their story further on, and to redraft it.

Once the first draft is down – and of course, this may take several days, weeks or even longer if the story is a full novel – then the next stage may be to trial run it. The writer needs to find out:

a How effective it is as a story (redrafting).

b Where the spelling, punctuation, layout and presentation need to be changed (proof reading).

Redrafting

Redrafting is not an easy skill. One of the problems is that when you have written something you read it as the writer – from that angle it may look fine, after all, you know what you meant to say. But what you need to do is to return to the piece of writing as a reader might. To distance yourself from the writing it could be put away for several days, or it can help to type it up on the wordprocessor so that it is no longer in your handwriting. Somehow this makes it easier to make changes, trim bits down, add in, etc.

✳ Some children will have orally redrafted the story as they told it, before writing. Some children redraft in their heads before they write the words down. Some write the words and redraft mid-sentence. Some complete several sentences and then go back over it and redraft. Some like to finish and then redraft. Some like to leave it for a while and can then return to improve their writing. Some of us do all of these at different times. There are no set rules for redrafting – only guidelines and suggestions. Each author needs to find their own way. If children are to develop redrafting techniques, they should be asked what they feel they need to attend to, before the teacher gets her two-pennyworth in.

The children will learn a lot about redrafting from their teacher (and from each other). The teacher should discuss each child's writing progress from time to time – keeping a careful note of the discussion and outcomes agreed. When focusing on a story look for **WHAT** has been written, and **HOW** it has been written.

WHAT – give an initial positive response, like 'This is an interesting start'. Ask some questions to get the author talking. Move on to identifying and praising all the things you like about this story, what it reminds you of and how you feel about it. Call over some others to hear it, and read some of it aloud. Look for:

a story that clearly, logically unfolds;
a story that intrigues you;
a story that surprises you;
a story that you can see;
characters that you can hear;
an exciting start that gets you straight into the action;
unusual and original ideas;
details that bring the setting, characters and action alive;
action that is well described;
a story with pace;
language that illuminates and brings the story alive;
a story where you can hear the author's own voice.

Having offered praise and helped the author to identify her

strengths, move on to help her consider places where development might be needed. See if the author can spot some areas for development – 'Are there any parts that you are not yet happy with?' Consider the story structure and the language used. Is the opening engaging? Is the scene clearly set? Can you picture the characters? Does the story drag? Is there a genuine problem which needs resolving? Does the action flow logically and clearly? Are there any parts that are red herrings and could be cut? Does the story hold your attention? Is the ending satisfying? Is the ending well thought out, or just 'and it was a dream'?

It doesn't help to highlight too many problems that might need redrafting. Concentrate on one, or two at the most.

You might also focus more closely on the choice of words. Are there repetitions? Are there too many adjectives ('the great, snarling, growling, well-groomed, savage, ugly dog')? Do some of the words mean the same ('the damp, wet, moist cave dripped')? Are there any overstatements ('the butterfly shot across the lawn')? Is there too little description so that we cannot see the story in our minds ('the tramp came down the road')? What we need to know is HOW that tramp came – was he running, leaping, jumping, bounding, hobbling, crawling, hopping? As soon as we know he was limping, we can begin to see him moving down the lane. Look for moments where the author has stated the obvious ('the wet water'), or has waffled ('I got up and wandered round the room and when I got over by the mirror I looked up and had a look and when I looked I saw'). Look for the use of 'ing', as sometimes this can be trimmed to bring about more dramatic impact. For instance, 'he was screaming' has more impact as 'he screamed'. The change brings the action alive. Suddenly it is happening, here and now. Watch particularly to see if the story is reported or created – does it tell what happened, or does it make the action happen on the page?

One final thought. Most teachers crouch over children's writing almost ignoring the child. The important place where we hope the learning will occur is in the child – not on the piece of paper. Perhaps we should angle ourselves towards the child as we talk together, remembering the value of listening.

Early writers should not be expected to launch into redrafting their work. The earliest stages call for the teacher to respond as an enthusiastic reader, writing down what has been written if the child's own mark-making is still at the scribble stage. Redrafting might begin as the teacher is scribing in front of the group – re-reading what has been written, maybe adding a word, changing a word, or altering the ending – demonstrating that writing can be changed for the better.

No one would expect the early writer to rewrite for publication – stories can be too long for that. However, if a wide margin is left, correct spellings can be inserted in it by the teacher. The child rubs out her incorrect spelling and changes it. She can practise 'Look, Cover, Write, Check'. The margin can be trimmed off and the spellings inserted in a spelling book. Redrafting can also be highlighted as we read story-books by pointing out – or asking for opinions on – well-used phrases and words. Another early help is to read children's work aloud and ask the class 'Which bits did you like best?' This helps them begin to identify strengths. Later on, you can ask 'Is there anywhere in this story where Mark might make a change?' This begins to help them identify weaknesses, but try to keep comments supportive, helpful and justified. Remember – we redraft when we are aware that the reader might not understand, we redraft to clarify, to put over an idea with more effect. Stories must have genuine audiences or redrafting becomes a pointless exercise.

It would be unreasonable to imagine that the sort of in-depth support outlined above could be given to every child. The teacher needs to be engaged in this whilst the children are writing. It is crucial that this time is fruitfully spent in this way, and not in walking round the room as the most highly-paid dictionary in your school! It is helpful to take stories home, read them at your leisure, make general notes and return them, reading out selections and asking what people liked or thought needed developing.

There are two other useful strategies at this stage – story groups and story partners. In a story group, each child takes it in turn to read their first draft out to the group and can then get a reaction and supportive suggestions. A story partner works in the same way. It is helpful to give children some ground rules for responding to each other's work, especially in the beginning. As they become better at it they will discover for themselves what is useful and what is not. A helpful response is one that not only leaves the author feeling OK about what they have written, but also one that helps to improve the piece of writing.

They should try to give the author an idea of how they feel about the story. Start by being positive. Tell the author all the things you thought were good. Then ask some questions about the writing. Try to locate one place where the writing might be developed. Discuss this. Leave the author to make up her own mind.

Some things to say:

'I like the beginning ...'
'What made you think of ...'
'These words work well ...'
'I like the bit where you said ...'
'This bit reminds me of ...'
'Tell me more about ...'
'Which bit do you like best?'
'Let's underline the best bits.'

Ideally, story groups and partners should help each other. After each session it is worth asking who found their partner or group useful and why. Try to get them to make explicit what was helpful.

HOW – Once the content has been decided upon, the spellings have to be checked, the punctuation established and, if appropriate, standard English established. Groups, pairs or individuals can work at this – underlining words they think are spelt incorrectly, looking spellings up in dictionaries or asking each other. The final check should be made by the teacher. This can be followed by plans for presentation – does the author want to publish as a book, what shape of book, what about illustrations, who will write the author's blurb, and who will review it once it has been published?

Much time needs to be spent on putting the book together, planning the layout of each page, decorating the cover and filling the inevitable gaps with designs and illustrations. Once published, a story that has travelled for so long and so far deserves to be shared. Read it aloud, read it to others, put it in the class library, send it to the Head, take it home, show it to Gran.

It is worth remembering that not all stories will get this far. At times they may be abandoned. However, once this sort of process is established you find that although less is written, the children are happier to work on it and find it more satisfying. They become authors. When authors visit their school, they too will know about writer's block, redrafting, checking the galleys for spelling mistakes, looking at the layout, pasting up the pages for the printers and the thrill of publication and being read.

General ways into story-writing

Advice from Jill Paton Walsh

- Here is a person I want to write about, what would this person do?
  or
- Here is an action I want to write about, what sort of person would do this?
- What kind of story you write is dictated by your own personality. Tell it the way you can, the way it feels right for you.

Advice from Roald Dahl

- It is essential to think of a strong plot. Work out the basic story before you start writing.
- You need a quick beginning. Get right into the story, otherwise people won't go on reading.
- You need to amuse your readers. Go for lots of laughs.
- Make up some extraordinary and unusual characters. Remember, ordinary people are dull.
- Have one or two very bad people in the story – and do them in at the end.
- It is important that the hero or heroine must win.
- Exaggerate and go overboard. Be daring with everything and when you have done that take it even further and be even more daring and more bizarre. And then go further still.

Advice from John Manwaring, 11 yrs

When I start to write a piece of writing I always build on a central idea. I prefer to work in quietness. If the piece of writing has to be good then I'm always concentrating. First of all I jot down ideas then I arrange them into the piece of writing. I then start to change words, I change non-interesting words for interesting ones. Make your work eye-catching and set it out so it looks good. Check for spelling mistakes. Never waste a good word, always try and fit it in. I like to read other's work and grasp ideas from it. Look at ideas from all sides and find their best meaning and use. Use words that fit well in the piece of writing. Never stop concentrating. Sometimes it helps to discuss your ideas with a friend.

Brief outlines – short extracts

- If you find that your class focus too much on the plot and just string a series of events together with 'and then', get them to write in stages. Alternatively, they could write just short extracts – beginnings, endings, parts of stories, or a series of linked extracts.

- Supply a character.
  Describe a character. Invite the class to make up a story about him or her.

- Supply an opening sentence.
  Out of the silence came a howl . . .
  She gazed into the darkness and screamed . . .
  Quick, let's get out of here . . .
  Stop!

- Supply the plot.
  Give the bare outline of the story, and let the class retell the tale. Or create an outline together.

- Give a list of titles to choose from.

- Give an ending:
  With that she turned and walked away from the king's palace.

- Use a photo, object or picture as a starting point.

- Organise the play corner to invite story-writing. Put out home-made, blank books and writing equipment, turn the corner into a cave, put out character costumes, leave a message from the king pinned on the wall . . .

Newstime warning

We began by considering the value of children talking about their own experiences. It is so easy in teaching to slip into habits. The Monday morning routine of collecting dinner-money while everyone draws a picture about their news and then writes a sentence underneath must be familiar to most infant children. Why a sentence? Why draw first and then write ... why not write first and then draw to illustrate? Does everyone have to write? Supposing some people haven't got much news, supposing nothing of significance happened? I remember Lawrence Cox, twelve years ago, handing me his news with a funny grin. It was about going onto the Downs with his mum and 'she was snogging with a stranger'. I reckon that he was so bored with trotting out the same sort of thing each week that he made up something a bit more spicy. Many children end up, if not repeating the same sort of news, at least repeating the same written structures. If you don't believe me pick up a news book and look –

This is me and Tom at the christening ...
This is me and Kevin flying a kite ...
This is me and Laura going to ...
This is me going to buy ...

Out of twelve news entries in this child's book, ten of them take the same form. Make news writing optional for those who really do have something they want to write down. Begin a newsboard, use a scrapbook, start a writing corner with little booklets, paper and writing equipment, put a letter box into the play corner and leave out some paper and envelopes, put some bills into the café, bring in an old typewriter, put an appointment diary beside the toy phone ...

With older children the routine of listening to news usually dies out. They become first-year juniors and suddenly home life is no longer a valued part of school. Try developing personal writing folders or journals. In these, they can write anything they like – a story, poem, something that has happened, something that is happening, something that is going to happen, something sad/happy/funny/dangerous, a secret they want to share. At first some will find little to say. This comes from several years of being told what to write about all the time. Gradually, a

33

self-confidence emerges in discovering that we can find our own starting points. The teacher needs to provide opportunities for children to select what they want to write about, as well as asking them to write to a set brief. In the folders it helps if they mark anything private with a capital P, and if the teacher only reacts with a comment.

'I was a brother except the other one died' wrote one boy. I didn't know that, and though we never talked about it I'm glad he had the chance to tell someone that poignant story.

In conclusion

This book is not a scheme. It hopes to provide some ideas and starting points for helping children develop as authors of stories. We have recognised the importance of bringing our own life stories with us when we sit down to write, of how we also bring the influence of the books we have responded to, and how the two weave together. This process takes time. The teacher's craft is in establishing a classroom environment within which children use stories to deepen their understanding of themselves and their world. It has nothing to do with text books, work cards and exercises. It has everything to do with the real engagement between an author, his audience and his world. I believe that we have to create communities of story-makers who grow together, for it is ultimately to do with discovering that stories have magic – and that magic comes from the story-teller within each of us. We should find and cherish that.

How to use this book

This book is intended to be a source of ideas and frameworks for helping children develop as story-makers. Our suggestion is that most children are moved too quickly into writing, and that there is much to be gained from:

a helping children develop as story-tellers;
b telling stories before writing them down;
c retelling stories and orally redrafting them before writing;
d giving time to the whole process of story-writing;
e sometimes abandoning stories and on other occasions publishing them;
f providing genuine audiences for all stories;
g encountering a wide variety of quality stories from the world family – both read and told.

In this book we suggest that children learn about how to write stories not only from practising writing them but also from telling, listening to and reading tales, and by responding to these in a creative way so that they make the stories they hear their own. Our ideas and approach have grown out of our own experiences of working with children and as authors. The most fruitful classroom circumstance emerges when children are viewed as authors, and story-writing is seen not as an isolated activity but as a co-operative venture – involving response partners, editors, proof-readers, book-makers and a genuine audience.

The book is set into six stages. The stages are not age-linked, and teachers will use those ideas that suit the needs of their class. However, the ideas do become progressively more demanding.

Each stage contains;

a a book (or books) to explore in depth with a class;
b a major writing project;
c a group of ideas for developing prose writing;
d a group of 'quick' ideas.

We expect that some, or all, of the ideas within a stage might form part of a year's work. Other starting points will emerge

35

from the children themselves, from local events, from topics under study and from the teacher's own inventiveness.

When selecting starting points we need to remember that in order for children to have a story to tell, they need to be able to relate the theme to their own experiences. The theme needs to act as a trigger so that the creative imagination can begin to construct and predict a sequence of outcomes to select from.

We envisage a classroom in which quality literature is shared, in which story-telling is a regular feature, in which story-writing is a respected process that leads to fruitful publication and, where appropriate, a place in the book corner.

Older children will need to develop the use of some form of journal or log in which to capture responses, ideas and impressions to do with their reading. This journal should also be used for writing ideas, suggestions, notes, lists, titles, beginnings, endings, characters, sketches, doodles, first-draft ideas, etc. Story projects and finished tales should be made into books and used as part of the children's reading.

Some schools may wish to use this book as a basis for building a coherent approach to developing story in their school. Many will not find such a strategy flexible enough, and will wish to pick and adapt according to how they perceive their children's needs. What should be emphasised is that teachers must leave as much opportunity for children's own starting points as for those given by themselves. Whilst it is true that an author may be asked to write to a brief, many will use their writing to discover their own stories and directions. However hard you try, you cannot write someone else's tale.

The teacher's skill may be in providing opportunities for children to find and celebrate the story of their own life. This is particularly important for those children whose home lives are chaotic. They need the sense of order a story might bring, and the sense of worth that comes in having their own tale recognised and valued. 'Storying keeps us at peace with ourselves,' says Chris Powling. Within the community of the classroom it may also build bridges of understanding to keep us at peace with those around us.

Pie Corbett and Brian Moses

Stage one

Mr Gumpy

Two of John Burningham's most popular books are *Mr Gumpy's Outing* and *Mr Gumpy's Motor Car*. In the first Mr Gumpy takes everyone for a boat ride, and in the second he takes everyone for a ride in his car. There are a wide range of activities that might arise from using the books.

Initial reactions

Mr Gumpy is an elusive figure. Explore questions such as: Who is he? Does he have a job? Does he have a family? How do you think he spends his day? Why does he let everyone pile into the boat? What might this tell us about him? Do you like him? Why? What is there about him that you like? Talking around the children's reactions to the story and pictures is an important starting point. Have you any questions about the story? Supposing you met John Burningham, what would you like to ask him?

Scientific activities

- Using tin foil or Plasticine, make a little boat that will float. How many toy farm animals can get into your boat before it sinks? Can you make a boat that won't sink?
  Try making a paper boat. What happens? How can you stop this happening? Test a collection of objects to discover which float and which sink. Can you make a floater sink? Can you make a sinker float?

- Load a toy boat with weights (eg unifix cubes). Whose boat can carry the most? Why do you think that was so? Suppose you put all the weights up one end: what will happen? How did Mr Gumpy's boat sink? How could you make your boat move along?

- How long might it take for clothes to dry? Test this by wetting some dolls' clothes – where will it be best to dry them? Try in different places – on a line, in the sun, in the shade, in a windy spot, on a wall, on the radiator, in the class. Which clothes get dry first?

- Make a tape of animal sounds. Can you guess which animal makes which sound?
- Design a bridge to carry a toy car across a certain distance.
- Make a model car that moves.
- On the carpet, decide where Mr Gumpy's house is, where the river runs, where the bridge is, where the road and track across the field are. Draw a simple map.
- How do you keep dry when it rains? What would make a good hood for Mr Gumpy's car? Test different materials to see which is the most waterproof.
- How can you get heavy things up slopes? Supposing the slope is slippy, what would help? Design and test some ideas.

Other activities

- Produce a collage of all the animals and the children and Mr Gumpy.
- Make an observational drawing of a member of staff's car.
- In PE, do some work on balance and staying upright. Also work on pushing and pulling movements. Use apparatus to practise climbing out of the water on to the bank.
- Sing 'Old MacDonald', 'Row, row, row your boat', etc.
- Write a menu for a summer tea.
- Draw an advert for one of Mr Gumpy's Mystery Tours.
- How do you know it's going to rain? Collect weather sayings.
- Collect anecdotes about long car journeys and breakdowns. Write them down. Invent a game for a long journey and share ones you already play.
- Look at the list of excuses the characters give for not pushing. What excuses do you use – at home, or in school?
- In *Mr Gumpy's Outing* each traveller is told they can come, but on one condition – for instance, the pig is told 'not to muck about'. Why is this funny? Supposing we took some wild or zoo animals, what conditions might we give them?

'May I come, please, Mr Gumpy?'
said the Chimp.
'Very, well, but don't monkey about.'

- Name Mr Gumpy's boat and car. Name the children.
- Pretend you are reading the news on TV. In groups work out how you would report one of the stories. Invent a newspaper headline.
- Use a dramatic improvisation to explore what the children say when they get home and tell their mum that they fell in. What will Mum or Dad say?
- We have the story of what happens when Mr Gumpy takes everyone for a ride in his boat and car. Tell the story of what happens when he gets out his hot-air balloon, his pony and trap, his minibus, or his tandem. Turn your tale into a picture-book.

If children are taking a closer look at a story and you are using the story as a starting point for a variety of activities, they will become familiar with the author and illustrator. The ideal situation is to have available a number of copies of the book you are using, and also other books by the same author. John Burningham is ideal as he has a number of excellent picture books that are fun and beautifully illustrated. Shirley Hughes, Anthony Browne, Ron Maris and Pat Hutchins are other authors to take a closer look at with young children. This may be the beginning of children's learning about one author/illustrator's style.

There may be a danger in trying to do too much with a story and it is possible to kill enthusiasm. There is no doubt that a sensitive approach is required to sharing stories. When planning activities it is important also to consider and follow the children's interests and suggestions, exploiting the learning potential within their own choices. If the class is engaged on a number of different activities, there is much to be gained from bringing them back together in order to present and talk about what they have been doing during that session.

Nico's world

Let us now shift our attention to celebrating a child as an author and look at some early pieces of writing by Nico. These range from his first days in school through to his first year in the juniors. Through this we may follow some aspects of his development as a 'composer' as well as discover some ideas for our own classroom use.

A typical early piece reads –

> We saw fireworks and sparklers and I heard a sparkler.

Early pieces tend to be reports of things done.

> One day I went to Emily's house and played.

He decides to use a typical story opening, but follows it by telling us his 'news'. The entry on the very next page uses the very same structure.

> One day I went to my Nan's and I played with my brother.

It is interesting to note that these pieces are written at the top of the page and followed by an illustration. He writes about his own life, offering comment, '*My brother is kind and he plays with me*'. All his early pieces are very brief. However, once he is given a scribe to work with and some fresh ideas that go beyond reflecting on his 'news', we see more of his ability to compose. Free of the overriding initial concerns with making marks on the page, he enjoys inventing some new ideas –

> I wish I was a tiger creeping through the jungle. I wish I was a grey elephant picking up logs. I wish I was a crocodile swimming in the water. I wish I had a red racing car that can jump over vans.

A week later the tiger re-emerges –

> I am afraid of a tiger creeping through the jungle trying to bite me. I am afraid of a ghost creeping at me. He is trying to eat me for his supper.

We could say that this is an early story. We have a setting, a character and something that might happen. A week later we can trace the same sort of structure –

> In my magic mirror I saw a tractor pulling a harrow behind dragging hops to the field. I saw a car just about to bump into another and they nearly fell into a fire.

The second sentence tells us the story of the car that nearly came to a nasty end.

The next session sees a sudden development. Nico writes a story that weaves his own experience with structures and ideas he has heard in his reading. For instance, those familiar with *The Hungry Giant* (published by Nelson) will know what a 'bommy knocker' looks like.

> I was playing with my toys. Mummy called. We went out to the fish and chip shop. I saw a giant striding through the street. He had a Bommy Knocker in his hand. He was going to knock the house down. We drove home in the car at top speed. We put the fish and chips in the boot. When we got home we ran into the house. The giant was not looking. He fell over. That was the end of him. We put our chips in the oven to warm them up.

He has used his own experience to construct the story as a whole, and has placed the giant within what really happened – yes, they did put the fish and chips in the car boot. The giant is appropriately dismissed, leaving the family able to complete their meal. The main difference here is that the scribe had time to listen and to question, so that the story could gradually unfold, with Nico occasionally re-reading what had been written. Already there is a growing appreciation of what a story might be about. His next story was even longer –

> We went to the seaside and the seaside was called Seasalter. We found some glittering shells. I put it in my bucket. Alex and Claire were there. When I put the shell to my ear it made a roaring sound. When I went home. I put the magic shell in my bucket. We went home. When we got home I got the shell out of the bucket and cleaned it. When I went to bed I put the shell under my pillow. In the morning it made a jingling sound. After that we went shopping. I left the shell at home. When we got home we had a biscuit. In the morning I got the shell out from under my pillow. I went downstairs and played with it. It had magic inside itself. When I looked into it I saw a shaped square. It was moving round and round. It was red and purple. It twinkled like stars. It made a Tailor lorry. I looked inside the shell and I saw pebbles and fruit inside the lorry.

Throughout his first year, Nico's retelling of news extends considerably beyond the earlier, brief sentences.

> One day Alex, Mum and I went to the swings and when I was
> on the top of a slope I got in the sleigh and went down it I
> went straight into a big snow drift and then we went home and
> had a cup of tea.

Again, we can see a simple story structure appearing quite clearly – the context is set, the main characters appear, the action occurs, something happens but it all ends happily. With this increasing fluency in the flow of ideas came an increased ability to retell stories.

> Once upon a time there was a sly-fox and one day he wanted
> to get a little red hen. In the morning he bounced out of bed
> and got his sack. Meanwhile the little red hen got some sticks
> and bought them back to her little house. Just then the fox
> saw what she was doing. When her back was turned the sly
> fox crept up the ladder and hid behind the door . . .

By now Nico had been in school for more than a year and had heard stories every day of his school life. His mum read with him every day, and the piece that immediately followed the above shows clearly how well he has caught the sound and structure of a story. Also he knows what a story is for. It is for telling . . .

> Chapter 1. You can read this story to the class. Once upon a
> time there lived a ghost, he lived in a haunted house. It had
> broken windows and lots of spider's webs. I went in the
> house. It was very spookey. The ghost said Come in. He
> slammed the door. 'Ha, ha, I've got you now.' I screamed . . .

As a first-year junior, he went on to complete a number of long stories – one which took over a term to write and turn into a book, complete with illustrations. I cannot quote from them for the simple reason that he has the books himself. However, the following piece is typical of his prose style, describing an illustration from a fairy-tale book showing a brick tower.

The deserted tower

> The grey dark sky hangs over the unsafe tower. The old dirty
> bricks crumble as the tower collapses. The rotting piece of
> timber has been used for thousands of years. The mouldy
> speck of moss spikes up towards the sky. The old fashioned

weather cock pointing out into unusual eternities. Three ugly
creatures scurry out of the pitch black doorway. What secrets
may be held in the enchanted tower? How many wars has the
tower survived? What memories does it contain?

By this stage Nico had begun to work happily with a response
partner, and was learning much about redrafting his own work.
He was slow at producing, but always carefully considered each
idea. This sometimes meant that the writing lacked flow (note
the way the first five sentences of 'The deserted tower' all begin
in the same way). However, he had begun to emerge as an
author. The following first draft he wrote one morning,
choosing the subject himself –

> The outrageous butterfly skims across the grass like a streak
> of lightning. Its deflectable wings reflect brightly on the
> morning sun. Its twinned shadow closes as the butterfly floats
> onto another land.

We might quibble with the overwriting, but here is a seven year
old beginning to experiment with words, unafraid of the
consequences yet also willing to sit and craft the results. He
wrote, 'I love writing because you never know what you are
going to say till you have said it.'

Now that I have read through all the pieces of writing showing
Nico's growth as an author, I have learnt a number of things
about his development. There seems to have been an important
parallel between his growth as a story-writer and his ability to
write his 'news'. He soon discovers what is worth saying in
'news'. What is worth sharing is a significant happening. It's
not worth recording that we had toast for breakfast, because we
have it every day ... unless, that is, Mum burnt it and the
toaster caught alight. He begins to select from his own
experience moments of significance, and retells them using a
basic story structure. At the same time he is managing to get
the sequence right and put in all the information we need to
understand what happened.

Alongside this growing ability, his story-telling begins. At first
he borrows structures (for example, One day ...) and then he
uses his own experience within which he weaves some story
elements – a giant, or a magic shell. He takes directly from

stories he has heard and read (eg bommy knocker) and begins to use these borrowed images within his own contexts. As his experience of stories grows, he becomes able to borrow, imitate and capture the appropriate style. It is significant that he can start a story with a written instruction to his teacher, '*You can read this story to the class*'. He knows that stories are for sharing and that his teacher may well read his story aloud for him. Through finding out that stories are significant and beginning to interweave his own life and his story experience, he is gradually finding his own voice as a story-teller.

To summarise the influences is fairly simple: a chance to listen to and read stories, a chance to tell stories from his own life, a chance to invent and share new stories, a chance to compose with support, a chance to take time, an approach to story-making as a craft, a community that is supportive of what he is trying to do.

Ideas for prose writing

Prayers

It's always struck me that the writing of prayers might be a fruitful area for exploring with children. Many of them hear and say prayers – sometimes repeating the same words so many times that they lose meaning. I well remember discovering that 'dellagud' actually was supposed to be 'Dear Lord God'! At about the same time it was pointed out to me that it was the Holy Ghost, not the Holy Goat ... this was, in part, explained by the ram's skull that was displayed on one wall in our local church.

At first, the prayers the children made up tended to echo the incantations they had learnt in church and assemblies. They adopted stilted language. We then moved to writing our own, trying to celebrate the things we liked. After hearing a prayer that the Navajo Indians used, Lisa wrote –

> Thank you god for all the beauty around us.
> May I live.
> For the rain, wind, snow, sun, clouds, snow.
> May I live.

For the sadness and happiness of life.
May I live.
For the families and people.
May I live.
For the beauty above me and the beauty around me.
May I live.
May I live.

Lisa Smith, 7 yrs

Later on, we wrote simple prayers to celebrate Harvest time.

When the wind blows and runs through corn, when the sea's spray lashes the fisherman's catch, when the Harvest moon rides in the night like a swollen balloon, when the apples are ripe and the mornings crisp we think of you and are glad to enjoy our world.

Mixed group prayer, 5–11 yrs plus teacher.

Everyday things

Writing is a chance to celebrate the thrill of experience – this is me, I was here and this is what it felt like. It is a chance to re-create the experience for others so that they may share in it. Small children are experiencing a range of everyday events that are new to them – going to the doctor, the dentist, having a haircut, riding a bike, going to London, going through the carwash . . .

My Doctor smells of soap and water. He walks quickly up stairs. My doctor is tall. His hands are cool and smooth. He touches me gently with a cold smooth stethoscope.

Timothy Greenhill, 7 yrs.

Such writing may occur during newstime or be carried out by choice in the writing area. Experiences that are common to most of the class might be focused on, talked about, described and written as a communal composition. There is the temptation to ignore everyday experience, as if to encourage children to write we need to do something 'imaginative' to 'stimulate' them. I have heard of teachers smashing bottles on walls, setting light to oily rags inside a dustbin, giving out handfuls of cold spaghetti for children to feel. My favourite was a supply teacher who brought two dead fish into school and got the children to feel and sniff them before writing.

It is not necessary to clutch dead fish in order to find something to write about. Every child's life is teeming with experiences that thrill, that frighten, that fill them with joy and plunge them into despair. Their worlds pulse with the excitement of their own activity, and we need to come close to their own sense of excitement, to discover what matters to them and to bridge the gap between their home world and school. There is no need to be writing stories about polar bears and penguins when the snow is thick on the playground and there is a smooth slide on the grass by the bike sheds. There is nothing to be gained from trying to imagine what it might be like to be an explorer in the jungle, when what you know best about is Bembom's funfair at Margate, because your dad works there on Saturdays.

As teachers, we have to rediscover our own sense of surprise and pleasure in the details of children's lives. Their interests may be teasing the woodlice out of the cracks in the playground wall, flying a kite in the park, skipping chants in the playground, playing Red Rover in the alley or kiss-chase in the snicket after school. Schools that ignore children's lives are saying, 'We are not interested in what you do, who you are and how you lead your life. That is not what school and learning is about.'

Outside my school the icicles hang down as thick as your arm. In the morning children would run in early to see them – and I had to persuade the caretaker not to break them off.

> The icicles hang from the gutter. They are slippery and cold. They are pointed. They are sharp as a knife. They drip. They look as if they are stuck together. You can see the light stuck inside them. They hang in a row.
>
> *Graham Wardley, 6 yrs*

Bubbles

Bubbles never fail to fascinate. In Cheltenham there is a huge clock in the arcade that has a giant fish suspended beneath it. On the hour music plays, a snake appears and chases a mouse, and as if by magic, bubbles blow out of the fish's mouth. Crowds gather every hour to watch. In the classroom, some simple science might be carried out to discover the proportion of washing-up liquid you need to water, to make bubbles. Bubble prints can be made, and bubble poems describing the swirling colours written.

Supposing I blew an enormous bubble and you stepped inside it. What might happen if we blew on to the bubble?

> I was blowing my bubbles and my bubble got bigger and I went up into the sky. I went up and up into the sky. And I saw a bubble Princess and I saw a bubble dragon and I saw a bubble Ted and I saw a bubble King and Queen and suddenly they all popped and it was a dream.
>
> *Helena Smith, 6 yrs*

This story is typical of the early author. It has a beginning that sets the context of what was happening, 'I was blowing my bubbles'. It tells us what happened next – 'my bubble got bigger' – and creates a situation to be resolved – 'I went up into the sky'. It tells us what happened in the sky – 'I saw a bubble Princess', and then produces a resolution – 'they all popped'.

Of course, the story is only there in a rudimentary form. It tends to report what happened rather than attempt to re-create what happened for the reader. Much of the action has stayed inside the author's mind and is not communicated. The determination and sparkle with which Helena read the story provides the clue that she can see and feel the action that these images relate to. She needs to move towards sharing more of her work with an audience, to tell more stories herself, to have the opportunity to make up stories without the problems of writing them down, and sometimes to plan the action ahead and write over a longer period of time so that she can focus on different parts of the experience each day. A response partner might help, by asking questions to show which parts need elaborating.

Secrets

> A secret always lies behind a face. As years go past it's like something that has disappeared forever.
>
> *Jessica Casson, 8 yrs*

Young children like the idea of being confided in, of holding close a secret, of being entrusted. You could say to them one morning, 'I have a secret that I want to share with you. Last night I found when I got home that ...' and spin a yarn. Perhaps your mum has turned into a poodle, maybe your cat can speak, maybe you are frightened of spiders and no one knows. Who else has a secret? Secrets can be real or invented.

> My secret is that I went to the fair and saw a cat watching us walking.
>
> *Lydia, 5 yrs*

Secrets should be shared in quiet whispers, perhaps into each others' ears. Form a line of children and whisper a secret down the line. How did it end up? Get one child to spread a secret – can it travel throughout the school? Tell someone a secret and make them swear never to tell anyone. Does it spread throughout the school?

Type up a secret message and post it to someone in the class. Put it in a simple code. Pin a secret up on the class notice-board, 'It's a secret that ...'

Wishes

In Ron Maris's book *I Wish I Could Fly*, the tortoise wishes he could do all the things that the other creatures can do – he wants to fly, to dive, to climb and to run. In the end he discovers there is something he can do that the other animals cannot. What would you wish for?

> I wish and wish I had a rabbit. I would feed it every day. I would call him Glider.
>
> *Hannah Clews, 5 yrs*
>
> I have a wish for a pony so I can ride. I cannot go to riding because Mummy has to look after my brother.
>
> *Daisy, 5 yrs*

It is fun to create magical wishes. These could be whispered into the teacher's ear during the day and collected in a book of wishes. Try telling the class that you met a gnome last night and he granted you three magic wishes. Can they guess what you wished for? What would they wish for? This fantasy is one that most children have shared ... a smile of recognition crosses their faces. One bright girl had found the answer to being limited to only three wishes. Her first wish was, 'that any wish I make can come true.' She'll be well prepared if she ever meets that gnome! Wishes in this situation tend to be for material possessions like money, wishes for family and friends, wishes to change ourselves, wishes for the world, and occasionally a crazy, silly wish, like 'I wish I was a slipper covered in mud that Dad thinks is a chocolate pudding.'

Stories could be written that use the giving of magic wishes and where it leads. Try beginning by retelling the story of Midas and how what seems to be a good idea can turn sour.

The magic ring

What would happen if you found a magic ring and put it on? There are many stories which feature magic rings, for example, *The Hobbit* by J. R. R. Tolkien and *The Magician's Nephew* by C. S. Lewis. There are also stories with magic doors to step through, pools to step into, crystal balls to gaze into, carpets to sit upon – and all open up the possibility of inventing new and different worlds.

This sort of session might start with the teacher as story-teller. 'You found a magic ring last night and slipped it on. In a moment you were standing in another place ...' Once you have told your tale, you could pass some magic rings round (polished brass curtain rings). What might happen if you put one on? Where might it take you? What could you see there?

> I put on a ring of danger and then a dragon came and I thought he was going to eat me up ...
>
> Celeste, 5 yrs

Though we never find out what happened to Celeste, her story creates a conflict and suggests what might happen.

Writing from stories

John Burningham's book *Would You Rather* is an open invitation to create your own options in the same vein:

Would you rather be chased by glowing were wolves, ride on a Father Christmas sleigh or be chased by a wild rabbit that tries to eat you up. Would you rather be locked in the cupboard by someone who has the padlock, be put in a rocket that soared up into space or be locked in a black car in the car park . . .

Serena, 6 yrs

The different options could each be illustrated and displayed alongside the writing. Pairs could ask each other what they would rather do. It will take a long time to erase the memory of children asking each other so seriously, 'Would you rather eat a worm or fall in some mud?'

Roald Dahl's *The Magic Finger* could lead to inventing what might happen if you had a magic finger that could turn people into things: 'I would change Mr Corbett into a tiger so he could growl all the time.' A magic finger could also be used to turn objects into different things. 'I would turn a stone into a cream cake', thereby avoiding the possibility of using the writing to be unkind and turn a classmate into something really nasty!

A picture book such as *The Snowman* by Raymond Briggs offers an ideal opportunity for children to invent their own storyline. A good moment for this would be when a new arrival comes to the school. Invite an older child to tell the snowman story. This gives a purpose and audience to the telling.

A reading of *Where the Wild Things Are* by Maurice Sendak could lead to telling each other about times you've been naughty and been sent up to your room. What might happen if you found yourself in the place where the wild things are? A story prop such as a stuffed wild thing toy might be used. Supposing our wild thing came alive?

Many stories that come in a series with a main character could be used for telling, taping or writing new tales about the character. In *Alpaca in the Park* by Rachel Billington, Alpaca gets lost. What would happen if Alpaca fell out of the shopping trolley in Tescos? A theme such as this might well link in with a private fear that many children have – being lost in a public place such as a supermarket.

Ron Maris's book *Are You There, Bear?* could be explored in drama with children hiding in the hall curled up, and one person creeping round with a torch searching for bear. Then seated in a circle, you might tell the story in the round of bear's adventures in the dark at night. How did he get out of the toy cupboard? An active and lively start to a story-telling session can be very useful. Once all the excess physical energy has been run off, the children may sit down ready for a quieter session.

Martin Waddell's book *Can't You Sleep, Little Bear?* might lead to talking about night-time fears. In the story the big bear is reading a book. Can you write the story in that book?

Sam had chosen to read the *Oxford Reading Tree* series, and was very taken with the idea of a magic key that could take you into other places and different worlds. He spent over a term carefully writing and ultimately publishing his own magic key story –

Once upon a time there was a lorry and there was a storm. A magic key fell out of the sky. The lorry went past a bridge and it was windy. The wind blew the key off the lorry roof into the sea. And a fisherman felt something heavy. It was very heavy. He thought it was a shark. He hoisted it in. He jumped. He was surprised to see a key that was heavy. He saw a box fall out of the sky. He had a look in the box. There was a message. It said, 'Put the heavy key in.' The man put the key in the box. There was a big crackle and sparks came. Suddenly he realized that the key had turned to gold and many different colours. He ran home with all his fishing gear. The fisherman and his wife went to sleep too. They had some children. One of the children was five and the other child was seven. They took the magic box with the key. They said I wish we could be smaller. There was a crack. It made them tiny as a mouse and the children wished the key fitted in the toy jet. There was a little flash. They tried to fit the key in the toy jet. The jet door swung open. The children climbed in it. They flew round the house. They landed on their bed. Then they opened the door. They got out. They wished they were big. There was a flash and they put the key back. They went to sleep. In the night a spaceship came. They went through the window – out, smashing it. The children woke up. The aliens asked if they could have the key. They said, 'You may.' The aliens came to the key. They took it and the spaceship flew out of the window. The next day the children's dad thought it was a dream.

Sam Clews, 6 yrs

51

I have included Sam's complete text in respect for his great concentration and dedication in completing the story. It is interesting to note that Sam became seven during the time he was writing the story and his younger sister, Hannah, was five. Because he found handwriting such a struggle he aimed for the minimum to put the story across – this meant careful selection of ideas and words. He could flesh the tale out by talking around the action and explaining. When he first arrived at school he was determined that he didn't like writing and was no good at it.

The main difficulty for Sam was that he found handwriting difficult, and spelling even harder. In his mind if you couldn't do either then you couldn't write. It took a long time to begin to persuade him that he could make stories up, and that that was part of writing. This story he chose to do himself and he would work on it at odd moments day in, day out. He would plan each double spread, what was going to happen and what the illustrations would show. We began by making the book, so that there was an incentive to carry on with the writing. Given this sort of support – access to someone who will show an interest in what you are trying to do, the chance to engage in a genuine story-making activity, the chance to try and fail without fear, support with the secretarial features of writing, it is possible for children to begin to shift their own self-image from someone who 'can't write' to being an author. I still have Sam's book and he is still asking for it back!

James Stevenson's *The Worst Person in the World* is about the most horrible man ever – he eats lemons for breakfast (and finds them too sweet) and knocks the heads off flowers! The story tells what happens when he meets a monster called Ugly who decides that they should throw a party. Roi combines his experience of that story with his knowledge about dinosaurs and echoes from *The Snowman* by Raymond Briggs –

> Long ago there was a dinosaur and dinosaur took me to dinosaur land he said we will have a party together and we will have some biscuits.
>
> *Roi Roe, 6 yrs*

This is typical of how emerging authors plunder the images

they know and mingle plots, characters and action – often with their own lives – to create new tales with echoes of stories held in their minds. They not only make new stories, but also are making the stories they already know especially their own by fashioning them within their experiences.

The list of writing possibilities from children's picture-books is endless. You can plan to share a story with children and find that they are not really sparked by it. On other occasions a story sparks off ideas as if the tale had been the key to unlock new possibilities and excite the imagination. Often the stories children hear, and the rhythm and pattern of the sentences, will reappear without anyone realising it's happening. I remember looking through the storybook of a six year-old in Wembley and noticing that almost every story began with a lonely child, living on top of a hill with two wicked aunts. Often the story would get no further than this setting. It was no surprise to hear that the class had enjoyed hearing Roald Dahl's *James and the Giant Peach* at the beginning of term. For some reason this image had particularly struck this girl, and she needed to revisit it again and again. There will come a time when a new pattern should be established with her. We may attribute this to a child's desire to fulfil some inner need, but the truth may be that she is checking back over the page to find how the story starts, and is just copying the spellings; or maybe she believes that that is how a story starts. She needs to be observed as she writes and to have the chance to read her stories aloud and talk about them. It may be that the teacher could intervene before she starts writing, using questions to lead her to find a new beginning and explore a different world.

Dreams

We spend a lot of time dreaming or day-dreaming. Just think about it – most of us spend hours running over little stories in our minds, revisiting what has just happened and predicting what might happen. Often our predictions stray from the possible and enter us into that realm of 'What would happen if ... I won the pools (even though I don't even fill them in) ... I was made headteacher ...?' Of course, anything can happen in a dream. Our two-and-a-half-year-old talks about her dreams as if they are real. 'I was with Coco (her uncle) and we went to the zoo.' You can invent or make up anything for a dream.

This sort of session should be preceded by a sharing-on-the-carpet-time, talking about our dreams and day-dreams. Some children claim that they don't have dreams so you may have to invite them to make one up: 'Just close your eyes. What do you see, what happens ...?' A starting point such as 'Supposing you were walking home and ...' can be useful.

My dream
One night I had a dream and I could fly and I would like to fly to Ibitha Then I flew home to tell Mummy all the good news that I saw and Mummy was excited and then mummy told me to fly to Austrailia and see the Kangaroos so I did go and see the Kangaroos at Austrailia.

Dominic, 5 yrs

Draw a story

This can be done individually or co-operatively. The idea is to produce a story by drawing what happens. It may be that the children begin by using one drawing and telling the story that goes with it. This could move on to drawing several pictures from the story, perhaps the beginning and the end. Later this could move on to showing a number of different scenes in sequence. I have found that it helps if the children decide on their story first, then you ask them which scenes from the story they are going to draw. This sort of activity is ideally followed by the opportunity to share their story-boards with others.

There will also be opportunities for story-making using felt cut-outs, using farm animals, with puppets, with clay models, with papier-mâché models, with dolls, in the play corner, and in the sandpit. Most children will naturally enter into creating stories around themselves and manipulating the models they play with, talking as they play. The teacher can suggest and prompt ideas: 'What would happen if ...?' 'Supposing we ...?' 'Look out, here comes a ...' 'But over there stood ...' 'Then she ...' 'We could make up a story with these ...'. If children are asked to talk about their play you can gradually create an audience for their story-making. 'Would you like to tell us the story you made up this morning?' Story-making moves from a private rehearsal and manipulation of a tiny world to a communication and creation between people.

An activity related to this idea is to take the pages from a picture-book with no words, mount them on card and cover them. Ask children, in pairs, to put the story pictures into an order and tell the story that goes with them. Depending on the pictures, a variety of different things may happen. If the visual sequence is strong, they will probably all end up with the same sort of sequence and slightly different texts. If the sequence is not so obvious, then you will end up with a wide variety of stories to be shared. There is an important point to be learnt – stories need not be fixed. Given the same setting and characters, different tales can be woven on different days.

Clockwork toys

This idea involves developing a mimed piece of movement to a story, then using the action for writing. It would need to be developed slowly over a number of sessions. The outline story is as follows.

The scene is set in a toymaker's workshop. Here comes the toymaker. She dusts down her toys. It is the end of the day. (The toymaker should walk round and take out the toys one by one and dust them down. You could have some puppets, soldiers, ballerinas, toy dogs, cats, mice, a policeman, etc.) Oh, here come some late-night customers. They want to buy a toy for their children. (The toymaker could take each toy out and demonstrate how it moves. The movement could be set to music. The children could be naughty and they leave the shop.) The toymaker shuts down the shop. (The toymaker could have a silly assistant who helps.) Oh, here comes Mr Brown to look at the toys. I wonder what he wants, he doesn't have any children. He doesn't even like children. (Mr Brown snoops around, looks at one or two toys, glances at the cash till and leaves.) The toymaker locks the shop door and goes home. The second scene is at night. Everything is dark and silent. But who is this creeping up to the shop door? He's switched on a torch. It's Mr Brown – and he's breaking into the shop. (Once inside Mr Brown takes each toy out in turn. He sets them off – and somehow breaks each one. At last he begins to force open the till. But he has forgotten the toy policeman, who comes alive and marches across the room, raises his arm and hits Mr Brown with his truncheon.)

Each part of each scene needs to be carefully built up, with the children involved as much as possible in deciding how the action will go – what the toys should be, who should come in, how they will behave, etc. This sort of play is fun to present for parents or as an assembly. There is plenty of scope for children to use the play for a variety of writing activities:

- The toymaker's assistant's diary entry for the day of the robbery.
- An advert for one of the toys.
- Draw a toy you'd like to build and explain how it works.
- A letter from Pinocchio who is wanting to visit the toymaker for a holiday.
- A newspaper report about the robbery.
- An interview between the toymaker and his assistant, and the local TV or radio crew.
- Retell the story from the view of one of the toys. As a way into this, get the children to decide which toy they will be. Explore in drama how the toys move, get the children to think about what the toys look like, and get them to talk to each other about how they feel, being sold off at Christmas-time. Once they have begun to talk and tell from their character's vantage point, they may be able to retell the story. Ask them to tell the story pretending that they have been sold to a new owner; her teddy bear wants to know what happened.

Quick ideas

April fool

A list of good April Fool's day jokes:

Put plastic bottles outside instead of milk bottles.
Put onions in Wendy's bed.
Wrap up a stone to make a big parcel.
Dress up as a ragamuffin and knock at front door and beg for money.
Stick a penny on path.
Put salt in coffee.
Hide John's trousers.
Stick a cup to saucer.

Judy-Jane McGuire, 7 yrs

The best April Fool's day joke I had played on me was when my brother-in-law left me a note to ring a certain number and ask for Mr Whale. He had some information about the hire car for my wedding. I rang the number and asked for Mr Whale. An icy voice from the other end said, 'You *do* know that it is April Fool's day, and that this is Whipsnade Zoo?' A good joke at your own expense should be enough to discover all the children's family jokes and tricks.

Posters and pictures

Use unusual posters and pictures to act as starting points for stories. Try to begin from what the children notice: 'What's happening here?' 'What might happen next?' 'Can you tell me the story?'

Finish the tale

It would be irritating if you did it often, but it can be interesting to stop a story and let the children complete it. Or when you have finished the story ask them to draw the part they liked best and write about why they have chosen that piece.

Crazy inventions and machines

Design a crazy machine, draw it and explain how it works – a sweet-making machine, a machine to help you in school, a machine to do the washing up, for example. I visited St Stephens Infant School in Canterbury just after it had been burnt down. The school had been rehoused. They were staging a tremendous Arts day, based around the theme of machines. There were children drawing, painting, model-making and dancing, and I ran a writing workshop. I worked with a class of five-to-six-year-olds. One boy invented a machine that would keep all schools safe, by putting fires out if they ever started. None of the children mentioned their own fire – but they listened with a most serious concentration.

If I were the boss

What would you do if you were the Headteacher, your mum, the Prime Minister, or the Queen?

Invisible

Suppose you could make yourself invisible. What would you like to do for the day? Tell the story of what happens.

Endings

Tell the class the end of a story. They have to work out the beginning. For instance, you might say, 'And when the giant sneezed, the gates of his castle blew open and the villagers ran down to the river. The princess was waiting for them in her long boat. "Quick," she cried, "He's coming." And with that they rowed downstream, leaving the giant lonely once more.'

New clothes

Bring in a special item of clothing. Dress someone up. Who is this person? Why is she here? What has she done wrong? How can we help her? Tell her story.

Tiny booklets

Make some tiny booklets. Leave them in the writing area. Suggest that they are elves' books. Could the children write a story for the elves?

Telephone

In my old classroom I had a telephone. This was very useful as I could arrange for my wife to phone up and ask to speak to one of the children with a message: 'This is the dragon's niece and I'm coming to stay. Are you all ready?' This produced some excitement. Recently, I was sitting in a play corner that had been turned into 'Noddy's café'. The terror of the class was serving his customers. I thought that I was managing rather successfully to keep out of the action and quietly observe. Suddenly he picked up the phone and shoved it towards me. 'It's for you,' he said. 'It's your nephew and he wants to come round for a meal.'

Stage two

The jolly postman

There can scarcely be a classroom in Britain that doesn't have a
few books by Janet and Alan Ahlberg. *The Jolly Postman* follows
a postman's day when he visits various story-rhyme characters,
dropping off a variety of correspondence. The three bears receive
an apology from Goldilocks, the wicked witch gets an
advertising leaflet from Hobgoblin Supplies Ltd, Giant V. Bigg
receives a postcard from Jack, Cinderella is sent a little book
telling her story from the Peter Piper Press, the wolf is sent a
sharp letter from Red Riding-Hood's solicitors and Baby Bunting
sends Goldilocks a birthday card and pound coin. The book is
made so that every other page is an envelope containing the
relevant piece of mail. It is an open invitation to imitate.

Before starting this project, it is an idea to share the relevant
stories with the class, so that they are familiar with the
references. This is not strictly necessary – indeed, our three-
year-old enjoyed the book without knowing all the stories
referred to – but there is no doubt that there is more to be had
from the book if the references are fully appreciated.

A list of other traditional tales should be drawn up, including
tales from other parts of the world that might form part of a
similar story. Once tales have been decided on, you have to look
for the letter-writing possibilities within them. For instance, the
Billy Goats Gruff might get their solicitor to write to the troll
who lives under the bridge because he keeps threatening to eat
them up, or they might receive a letter advertising some new
horn polish to 'put the bounce back into your horns:
particularly effective against trolls'. Groups should work out a
basic story-line that can thread the pieces of mail together. This
might be plotted with a flow-chart. One group member might
write the main story, whilst the others draft copies of the
different letters, adverts and postcards. One of the main interests
in pursuing such a project is that it provides an ideal
opportunity for a variety of different writing modes to be
explored:

Simple telemessages:

TIME RUNNING OUT STOP GO HOME STOP FAIRY
GODMOTHER

For a telemessage, explain that the children can only have a
limited number of words – or give them a budget of, say, £1 and
charge them 10p a word.

Postcards:

Dear fairy godmother,
I am on holiday with the prince in a palace. We will buy you a
present. It is a jar of flowers. We will see you soon.
Love Cinderella.

Blank postcards can be bought, so that a message can go on
one side and a drawing on the other.

Informal letters:

Dear Mum Pig,

Having a good time. Got married, had two piglets. I have got a wolf
fur coat for you. Good hotel made out of brick.
From Little Pig.

Mud Cottage
Swamp Road,
326 BRL.

Dear Mr Troll,

Sorry for running into you with my big horns. I wanted to get to
that green grass and you wouldn't let me. Perhaps in future you can
let my family through. Would you like to come to tea? You can have
grass sandwiches. On Sunday.
From Big Billy Goat Gruff.

Formal letters:

To The Ugly Sisters,
6 Castle Paladium,
Manchester,
CT6 7ST.

Dear Ugly Sisters,

On behalf of my client Miss Cinderella I have been informed that you are giving her your dirty work. You are not allowing her to do things. If she tells me any more, I shall take you both to court. So, I should watch out.

Yours sincerely,
Mr Humpy.

To Mrs Witch,
Sweet House,
Dark Forest,
C6 72 HOP.

Dear Mrs Witch,

My clients, Hansel and Gretel, are telling me that you attempted to put them in the fire.

I am accusing you of attempted murder. I will be taking you to court on January 11th.

Yours sincerely,
Mr Dumple.

The work should be carefully drafted and checked. Formal letters will need to be typed. Younger children may need the assistance of older and more skilled book-makers, to collaborate with when making the books up and ensuring that they have the 'envelope pages' in the right place. These books offer an invitation to open them up and read. You'll find that the children soon go beyond inserting mail items and put in tickets for the bad wolf to go to a football match, passports for dragons, appointment cards for princesses, recipes for witches' spells, shopping lists for ogres, a vet's bill for the castle cat ...

If the children are to catch the appropriate tone and language they will need to hear several examples of the mail item. Having said that, we were surprised how easily and quickly they seemed to be able to write solicitors' letters. Surely, not all of them had received a solicitor's letter already? They enjoyed acquiring and using a new tone in which they were playing an adult role.

This sort of creative entry into a story deepens children's understanding of the story and its themes. It is another way in which they can play an active role in creating their storyworld. This particular book is unique in that there is the initial storyline of the postman, then the extension of a number of other stories, and finally the children's own creations in response. It is a multi-layered text which can be returned to again and again as children's reading experience grows. The other important element is that the humour appeals to adults, too – it's almost as if the Ahlbergs have slipped in some jokes for tired teachers at story-time and weary parents at bedtime!

The magic box

I first used this idea while running a writing workshop with top infants in Croydon. We sat on the carpet and began to mime our own boxes – some were small, some tall, some square, some round. Now where was the key? Ideas were suggested and once we had found the key, we opened the lid. What was inside? We mimed for each other, and guessed what each box held. I then suggested that the boxes might be magic. What could you find in a magic box? Perhaps you would find something completely impossible. At first, the children suggested some rather ordinary ideas – a bicycle, for instance. 'No, no,' I said, 'you could fit that into a large box. Think of something totally impossible.' Soon ideas began to flow – a cloud, a whole school, the sun, the night-time, a box of laughter, a box of sadness. Once their ideas were flowing, I suggested that they moved to the edge of the room and worked in small groups, using an adult to help with the writing.

In my magic box I had a sandstorm trapped and there was a man trying to escape . . .

This theme seemed to strike a chord, so later at school we explored a whole topic on the theme of magic boxes. Our ideas included:

1 Bring in a box from home. Tell the children that they have found the box and inside it there is some magic dust. What can the dust do? Write the story of what happens.

> One day I met my Mum. My Mum found a box. It had magic. It made me little. I went to a dead world and there

were men fighting. I was growing big again.

Paul Doogan, 5 yrs

Magic dust can be used in drama/movement sessions. Sprinkle dust to make the children move slowly or quickly, or to change them into someone else.

Alternatively, you find a box. You open it. What is inside? What happens?

> I found an old box on the beach one day. It was a bit rusty. It looked like it had been in a volcano. The lid was already open so I looked inside it. There were lots of things in it rustling and bustling about. They sounded like very nasty things inside. I rammed the box tight in case the nasty wonderous things may get out. Their eyes sparkled. They howled and bit at the box but of course they could not get out for the lid was shut.
>
> *Nico Van der Wurf, 7*

2 Start a box collection. Choose a box and draw it. Describe your box.

> It has a pocket book of spells in it. It is made of brass. It is made in the year 100. It has a glass top that guards the book of spells. It is a magic box. If it touches your cheek you turn invisible. If you say HAZANE CARANE you will turn into any animal you want to. If you say MORALE COLLENTOO you will have the speed of 1000000000000000 miles per second.
>
> *Mark Sheppard, 7 yrs*

3 Write a wish and place it in a box. Everyone takes another person's wish out. Or, write a secret and place secrets in the box. Take someone else's secret out.

4 Mime escaping from a box. Be a jack-in-the-box that comes alive.

5 Draw an island map and plot various features on it – lagoons, mountains, etc. Singe the edges to make it look old. Try warming the map in a hot oven to crinkle it slightly. Play a coordinates guessing game – like battleships – in which your partner has to guess where you've buried your treasure.

6 Write the story of someone who finds a treasure-chest. The treasure turns out to be something unusual. Discuss things that are 'precious' to us – they don't have to be material objects. What are our everyday treasures? What does it mean when someone says that you have been 'a little treasure'?

7 You are shipwrecked and only have a few minutes to climb on to the raft. You can take ten items from the sinking ship in your sea-chest. Each group has a list of twenty items. You have to decide which ten would be most useful. Another way to do this is to give each item a weight – you can only take a certain weight on the raft, or it will sink.

8 Write a day's diary entry for a newly-shipwrecked person.

9 Your class is going to bury a time-capsule not to be opened till you leave the school. You can put an object in. What would you place in the capsule and why? Or, you have to select a piece of writing from all the work that you have done this year. Which piece would you choose and why? Share it with your class. These pieces of work might be mounted on card, covered in sticky-back plastic and placed in a time-capsule box for others to read.

10 Find a sturdy box to make a soapbox. Everyone writes a suggested title for a short talk, then takes it in turn to choose one, stand on the soapbox and talk for a minute. Who can keep going? With this sort of activity, it is worth remembering that children get better with some practice. It also helps if once they have chosen their title, they have some time to jot down things they might talk about, and to practise in groups.

11 Design a package to keep an egg safe. Design an Easter-egg package. Design a package that will keep a biscuit dry. Investigate various packages from the supermarket.

12 Read 'The Three Little Pigs'. Build walls of straw, of twigs and of bricks. See how well they stand up to the huff and puff of a hairdrier. What do you think will happen? What did happen? Why do you think this is so? (You may find that the straw wall works best, and the bricks fall over.)

13 Create a display out of cardboard boxes placed on top of each other, with drawings and writing on the surfaces that face outwards.

14 The computer software company 4Mation has a very useful package for juniors titled 'Box of Treasures' which has an ideas booklet. Some of this would be suitable for younger children.

15 Place a 'special box' in the writing corner. Each day you could put into it a new object.

The Silver Watch
The back is smooth and round. It has hinges to open it. It has a gold wheel that spins round. It has springs. The spring beats out and in like a heart. It has a silver plate with patterns. The patterns are curls. The best part I like is the gold colour inside. The time is quarter past six. That is all I know of the Silver watch.

Steven Merner, 7 yrs

One day I placed inside the box a small, round box that had a unicorn painted on the lid. This fascinated Deborah:

The graceful unicorn, trapped in a world of varnish, skipping among the daisies trapped on the elegant blue box.

What has the box ever held? A diamond. A ring. A heart of rubies. Or a unicorn with a sapphire collar. The inside of the box is as black as ebony. The unicorn can never feel happy or sad. The unicorn is trapped between both, never will he move again. The person who owned the box was a merchant who staggered around. The merchant rode a golden camel. The box was his favourite possession. Yet only he knew what it contained. He passed on the secret to me. Inside the box was a key, a key to let the soul of the unicorn out into the world . . .

Deborah Blanchett, 8 yrs

16 Create an imaginary box. What might the box be like, what might it contain?

Dale created a coffin:

On the coffin the gory carving seems to be living, the great serpents head seems to sway like a cobra hypnotising its prey. The coffin holds anger and hatred that squirm around entwining themselves together forming a huge ugly mass of anger and hate.'

Dale MacDonald, 7 yrs

Ideas for prose writing

A fungus foray

If your school is near enough to damp woods, wait for autumn and the fungus season. Invite a band of parents, and kitted out with plastic bags and containers, set off on a 'fungus foray'. Samples should be collected with care – reference books should be used so that you don't collect anything poisonous, and appropriate warnings and exhortations given. **Wash your hands when you get back to school.** On returning to the class, microscopes, lenses and magnifying glasses should be ready. This should lead to identification, displays, mapping the route taken and the various finds, observational drawings, paintings, printing, spore collection and writing descriptions.

> The soft, browny-white, frail gills of a toadstool, standing in the damp, gungy wood. It grows wildly in the wood. A wind springs up. It blows a sycamore seed off onto the toadstool. The gills cling onto the domed cap that is supported by the long stalk that thinly winds up to the control room of the mushroom. The curved ring that is very floppy. Cracked top with different shades of brown. A very dark brown on the middle. It smells like an ordinary mushroom. Sliced gills look as if they have been sliced in half by a knife.
>
> *Ralph Wood, 8 yrs*

Skull and cross bones

Young children love making collections – feathers, leaves, stones, shells, buttons ... and bones. Our collection of bones was started by the skeleton of a barn owl borrowed from the local museum service. This lead to rabbit skulls, a pig's skull, various unidentifiable bones, a pair of antlers, a squirrel's skull and birds' wings. One day Abby said, 'I've got a killer whale's skull at home.' 'Nonsense,' I retorted, thinking that she was having me on. But sure enough the next day Bernie brought in a huge skull that they had found off the coast of Scotland, one holiday.

Drawing is a useful way into writing. It provides an opportunity for close observation, to see the details, to notice.

> The jagged teeth are like the hard side of a mountain. The lifeless skull as it sinks down into the soft muddy earth. The smooth crest pushes its way out of the dead skull.
>
> *Nico, 7 yrs*

Reference books can be used to identify and label skulls for display.

The iron man

Some interesting writing can arise out of making junk models, then writing about them – designing an advert to sell the model, or writing its story. Richard wrote the following piece after we had read *The Iron Man* by Ted Hughes together and his group had built a huge shiny Iron Man with eyes that flashed. He wrote it at home, typed it up on his mum's typewriter and pinned it on to the class newsboard.

> **The Metal Man**
>
> His metallic arms tower over the derelict building. His twisted wires and golden circuits glint in the rising sun. The silver steel crushing legs attached to his golden body and his bold metallic chest bulges like a pigeons breast. His eyes are a glaring greeny colour and glance over the brick red roofs and the torn chimneys covered in soot. His massive legs boot the poor people as if they were tiny stones. His solid knee caps ram the moulding brick work. The people shriek as the brick and moulding rubble come hurling down, smothering their bodies. A frightened lady sits in an armchair. She's full of fear. The echoes of yelling people sprinting away from the metallic monster. His spikey fist shatters the filthy windows and rips the curtains. Then he ponders on devastating as he prowls dangerously. All that is left is the frightened lady lying on the rock and rubble.
>
> *Richard, 7 yrs*

Secret places

Nearly all of us have secret places. I used to have a secret hole in the wall beside my bed at home. No one else knew about it except for me. I hid pencils, bits of important paper, shiny sweet wrappers. Children have secret and special places in cupboards, under bushes, on waste ground, in derelict buildings, by old railway sidings, in tumbledown shacks . . . often in the places where they are not supposed to go! I've never asked children to write about their own, real secret places. Somehow it seems that you might be in danger of stealing the secret from them – but we have written about the secret places in our minds, the lands we inhabit when we day-dream.

My Secret Garden

It was a beautiful spring morning and I opened the creaky door. I wandered in and gazed at the forgetmenots which were deep purple and cool blue. Tendrils surrounded the wall and ground. There was a sweet scent. Bees were humming while wasps sucked nectar from gold, pink and snowy white begonias. Birds perched on the plum trees singing a fantastic song. Apple trees were in bloom. They were a creamy white with lightish lilac sprays. A stream was flowing by splashing red, orange and glowing orange wallflowers. Butterflies gleamed in the bright sun.

Kerry, 7 yrs

The garden is a powerful image in literature. What might happen if you wander into this paradise? Supposing you went into the garden and stole something? An interesting passage to read is the section in *The Magician's Nephew* by C. S. Lewis when Digory enters the garden where the fruit that will bring his mother back to life grows. The witch tempts him to use the apple to save his mother but bring about the downfall of Narnia. Special gardens also appear in *The Secret Garden* by Frances Hodgson Burnett and *Tom's Midnight Garden* by Philippa Pearce.

Homelife

Write simple descriptions of home activities – clearing the drains, washing up, peeling carrots, polishing the table, things Mum gets me to do. Or observing actions of others at home –

> Slowly and carefully Mum irons the jeans, skirts, socks, shirts
> but in the corner the washing machine grumbles, mumbles,
> moans and tumbles. In the sink my sister is doing the
> washing. She strangles the washing. It twists like a screw.
> She hangs it up. It hangs on a post. Then she dips her hands
> into the boiling water. She picks out a shirt. She squeezes it
> hard as if she is strangling her victim and putting him in a
> cage. Once again she hangs it up on the line to dry.
>
> *Nigel Hoad, 7 yrs*

Nigel is moving to a stage where he needs to trim down some of the lists of words he can think of, for example 'grumbles, mumbles, groans and tumbles'. He can brainstorm quickly and has a range of words at his command. Unfortunately, some of these verbs clash against each other and Nigel might need to select which he feels is the most appropriate. He lists the words because he knows them and can use them – now he needs to move on to consider the reader. It is often useful to leave a gap between the writing and the redrafting – or to return to a piece of writing several days later. Read the piece out to the child so that they are in the position of being the reader. This makes it easier to hear what you have written as a reader might, rather than as the person who has just written it.

Nigel's piece also attempts to re-create the experience. It is more usual for young children to write about home life in an anecdotal style –

> One day in Lewes where my Dad was putting the floor-boards
> down. He had only three more floor-boards to put down when
> he ran out of nails so he went downstairs to borrow some off
> my grandad who was working downstairs. My grandad lent
> my Dad 12 nails (I counted them). Then I went upstairs again.
> When my Dad had finished nailing all the floor-boards down
> he heard a faint mewing noise. He bent down, pulled a floor-
> board up and a tabby cat leapt out and my Dad and I burst out
> laughing.
>
> *Dale MacDonald, 7 yrs*

Bumps in the night

There are various ways into this idea. You could tell the first part of the story and leave the children to use their writing to find a solution, or to discuss in groups and present an ending. The story outline is quite simple. You are woken up at night by a noise downstairs. You creep down to see what is going on and when you get there you find that something has happened. Children suggest a wide range of possibilities – burglary, a stolen chocolate cake, an open window and a figure running away across the garden, the flat door open and the sound of footsteps echoing down the corridor...

The Case of the Missing Jelly Babies

One night I woke up, a strange noise was coming from the kitchen. It sounded as though someone had moved the record player into the kitchen and had put on my Adam Ant record. I crept down the stairs and looked into the kitchen and there were jelly babies dancing to it. When they saw me they turned off the record player and as I entered into the kitchen they backed away. I began to advance more quickly. I started to chase them round the kitchen and one by one I caught them. I put them into the packet, sellotaped the top and put them on the top of the sideboard. I quietly crept upstairs and then I heard a noise. It was a jelly baby following me upstairs. I picked him up and ate him.

Kerry Colbran, 7 yrs

When working on a group solution, it is helpful if each group selects someone who will report back. A time limit helps them keep to the point. For this sort of activity allow ten minutes if they are not used to group problem-solving, building up the time allowed as they can cope with more. It is a good idea to help establish good group behaviour by getting groups to identify why they worked well. What sorts of comments are helpful? How can you include everyone? Is it fair if one person does all the talking?

A monster in school

Your first response to this title may be, 'Yes, I've got several in my class', but that is not quite what I was thinking of! Again, the teacher can provide the starting point that gives the children a problem to solve. Basically, a monster appears somewhere in the school – what happens next? Monsters could appear in the bikesheds, a large egg could be found in the stock cupboard that hatches into a tiny dragon, a member of staff could turn into something nasty, or you could draw a monster on the board that comes alive when your back is turned, slithers off the board and eats someone. How do you capture it?

BlubbleBlob the Monster

It was early Friday morning. Mr Corbett had just drawn a purple, oval shaped monster on the board with one eye in its proper place, one where its mouth should be and one where its chin should be... Mr Corbett had gone out of the room to have a talk with Mr Fountain. Everybody was looking at the blackboard. When. When. It blinked. Yes it actually blinked. Nobody else saw it, just me, Just I saw it blink twice. It blinked at me. Why, why me. I opened up my pencil case and threw a pair of scissors at it. Then just as I was about to laugh it jumped off the blackboard. Well Mr Corbett hadn't coloured it in and so the scissors went right through the ignorant beast of a picture.

The beast or rather, Thing. Had crawled over to Kerry and being as it was only a small little thing Kerry was too big...

I knew I must of been barmy. Really. But somehow I felt sorry for it. Well, I felt silly but I felt sorry because it wanted some food and he was too small and everybody in the class was too big. Then I remembered some jelly babies in my bag.

I crept out of the classroom and the thing followed me. I was just about to give the thing some jellybabies when, I heard laughter coming from all three classrooms and there was Mr Corbett running round the central area with my pet thing following him...

'Help oh Help.' 'Deborah you rat get him off me.' Shouts Mr Corbett. Everybody was laughing. But Mr Corbett wasn't...

Then I had an idea...

Deborah Blanchett, 8 yrs

This is an interesting story because it shows Deborah's earliest attempts to use paragraphs. She also uses the jelly babies from a previous story-telling session, borrowed from Kerry. When I read the story I can hear Deborah's voice telling it – it is a real story, being told on to the page. She is telling it to someone in her mind as she writes. She is listening to her own inner story-teller. And she uses her punctuation in an original way to work for her, to give the story effect – *'The beast or rather. Thing.'* She puts the full stop in as a clear indication that the teller should leave a dramatic pause before the word 'Thing'. She uses a capital letter for Thing to indicate that it should be emphasised . . . and she presses harder with her pencil, making a darker mark on the page. Indeed, it is almost as if she is using her marks on the page as a story script for someone who will read aloud. These are important signs that she is beginning to use the conventions to gain effect. She is controlling the language and its presentation to communicate how she wants to tell her story.

Traditional tales

Traditional tales, told and read aloud from different cultures, are an essential ingredient in creating a story world that meets children's needs and enriches their lives. In many ways such stories should be told – because that is how they have been handed down and shared, sometimes over many centuries. They are part of the oral tradition and their magic power may partly lie in the differences between telling and reading aloud. There are a number of fairly recurrent elements: hovels/huts/cottages; castles/palaces; songs/rhymes/riddles/spells/incantations; evil/good characters; forests/woods; lakes/ponds/mirrors; a drop of blood; aunts/uncles/sisters, etc.

Common elements could be listed, using children's suggestions, and children invited to create their own traditional tale. A useful reminder is that at the start there is often someone who is down on their luck, someone who in order to be happy is set a number of tasks, someone who is kidnapped or imprisoned, someone who becomes enchanted. . .

The writing of such stories demands that they be told and read aloud, shared with other children in groups, made into books and preserved for the class library. The selection of key features and 'symbols' within the stories may sometimes seem to be of significance if the children are using their reactions to explore genuine needs.

The Reed Girl

Once upon a time there lived a Queen and King. The Queen

was not a happy Queen because she did not have a single baby or animal. One day a baby boy was born to them and the Queen was very pleased with her newborn baby and the newborn baby was very pretty indeed. One day his mother was knitting a jumper for her baby boy. Just then his mother did something with her sharp needles she pricked her finger and three drops of blood fell upon his mothers knitting. A few days later she died and his father looked after him very well indeed. When he was eighteen he said to his father please can you show me the way to the three reeds where the three pretty girls are? So the King said to his son please do not go to the three reeds but he would not obey his father. At dinner time he would not come down to dinner because he was packing for his ride to the three reeds. In the night he set off to the three reeds. When he got to the three reeds he cut down the first reed with his sword and a lovely girl stepped out . . .

Lisa Smith, 7 yrs

In the story Lisa takes an idea she has heard before from a tale by Joan Aiken, where the prince is told, 'in one of those reeds is hidden a girl on whom the starry sky would gaze with smiles'. She weaves her tale, adopting the style of the traditional tale – 'One day a baby boy was born to them', 'three drops of blood fell', 'and his father looked after him very well indeed'. Laced in with the tones of the tale are elements of her own home experience – 'his mother was knitting a jumper', 'he would not come down to dinner because he was packing'. Lisa seems to have reached a transition stage in which she can adopt an appropriate tone and style, yet mingles this with phrases that do not quite fit. She is moving towards the ability to adopt another language depending on the writing style required, and this she has gained through hearing stories, reading stories and telling stories. A useful next step for Lisa would be to share her story with her writers' group or response partner. They might be asked to list some questions about anything in the story. This might help Lisa identify parts of the story that need clarification – for instance, what is the significance of the three drops of blood? Do they relate to the three reeds?

Traditional tales are also useful as starting points for dramatic exploration. For instance, the King has ordered all the toymakers in the land to visit his palace. When they arrive, he demands that they make a toy for the prince and princess. The teacher can take the role of the king's adviser and the children become the toymakers. From this beginning there are many possibilities to explore. In pairs ask each other who you are, where you come from, what sorts of toys you make. How do you feel coming to the great palace? Describe the great hall. The King's adviser could read aloud the King's decree. In groups, discuss some ideas for toys. What would a prince/princess like? List 'boys" toys and 'girls" toys. Just at the point when the children have decided that the princess should have a 'girls" toy, pretend that an envoy has arrived from the King saying that he will throw anyone in the dungeon who decides on a toy that the princess dislikes. What might this princess be like? What sorts of toys do you like? Do all girls like dolls?

This project could lead into designing and making a toy, packaging the toy, presenting the toy to the King, trying each other's toys out, and writing a report for each other.

Retelling tales

A straight retelling of a story might be a very dull exercise – after all, why retell the story when we've only just heard it? However, there may be some mileage in re-creating stories in a variety of different ways for different audiences, in order to make the story more our own and to explore its themes more deeply.

- A simple way to encourage retelling of tales is to tell the class a story; during the day they have to pass it on to as many others as possible. A visit to a younger class could provide an opportunity to tell the story to a small group of younger children.

- Stories can be re-created in picture or storyboard form. The boards have to hold the main scenes from the story. Groups can decide which scenes should be represented, and write the story that goes with the board. This would naturally lead to making a presentation.

- Stories can be reproduced in simplified cartoon form. Again, the aim of such an activity might be to create a book for younger children.

- Stories could be retold in the round with each child taking it in turns to tell the next part.

- After the teacher has told the story you could ask the children to list questions that they'd like to ask one of the characters.

- Crucial parts could be re-enacted.

- Characters from the story could be interviewed about what happened or could retell the story from their viewpoint.

Initially you may have to take a strong lead in this sort of activity, gradually stepping back as the children 'get the idea'. The piece below is the retelling of Moses parting the waves by a bystander.

The Red Sea

The roaring waves hurtled back and with a gasp the foam raced to the shore spitting and rushing through the sand. Like the crack in the ground of an earthquake. The Wizard spoke to the Pharoah's soldiers then to the sea which moved at every word. The Wizard did not speak to the sea in the same language as he did to the soldiers but he spoke slowly and calmly to the sea which parted as no man could imagine before. The strangers passed through as a band marching through the town.

But now the strangers were running from the chariots, from men with horses who were racing through the pathway in the sea pursuing them.

When the strangers reached the other shore the wizard spoke to the sea. And the sea closed. The men and their chariots could not race forwards. They tried to run back for safety.

But once more the sea closed like the lips of a man yet it did not speak.

Deborah Blanchett, 8 yrs

In comparison with Deborah's story 'BlubbleBlob the Monster', this is a completely different use of language. It is not so directly anecdotal. She has adopted another voice and a more literary style.

Another way into retelling tales is to ask children to go on a storyhunt – they have to find a story from home, from Mum,

Dad, Gran, next door, and then bring it back to share. The story could be a tale from someone's life. An interesting stimulus for such a session is to ask the class to bring in a favourite or special object from home – a photo, letter, holiday gift, first tooth – and then tell its story. These sessions rely on placing an emphasis on the significance of our own lives. We all have many stories within our own experience, and some hold a lot of importance for us. As we share anecdotes we re-create the experience for ourselves and for others – we relive the moment, but from a safe distance. The words contain our emotions. It is worth the teacher sharing her own anecdotes, and such sessions may work best in small groups so that the large 'class audience' doesn't inhibit. It is important to emphasise that whilst someone is telling a story, everyone else has to become a good listener. Some interesting, reflective writing might follow such a session.

> I enjoyed this mornings story session. Joanne told about her gran who got cancer and died. My Mum's friend died but I never told about it.
>
> *Tim, 7 yrs*
>
> When it was my turn I felt really scared that I might forget. But I found it easy because I knew what happened.
>
> *Sally, 7 yrs*
>
> Anneka spoilt it because she kept talking.
>
> *Julie, 7 yrs*
>
> In our story session I told about my Mum's Dad who had been a miner. He had mined for gypsum. He said that there were great caves of it and that it gleamed all white. He was hit by the train that they had underground. He couldnt hear it because he was deaf.
>
> *Sydney, 7 yrs.*

Parents and friends could visit the class on a special occasion to tell stories and share their own life stories. Sometimes the most ordinary people have locked up inside them the most remarkable tales (see the story of the boat people in the final chapter). Anecdotes help us make discoveries about each other, and broaden our view.

Teachers' stories

For a fortnight each teacher chooses a story to read and the children are allowed to go and listen to any of the stories. So that numbers are balanced, they have to choose and stay with their choice. The alternative to this idea is for teachers to decide on a 'storytime' and visit each other's classes as visiting story-tellers/readers.

An extension of this is to invite colleagues to write about early memories such as 'What was it like when you were at school?'

Our School Canteen was an old hut and the prized seat to occupy was by a window so that at a judicious moment one's dinner could be shot out of the window!

Mr Fountain

My first memory of school occurred on the second day in the infants. Somehow or other I managed to get a piece of chalk stuck up my nose. Obviously at that age I thought it would be stuck up there for ever but my kind teacher removed it with a pair of tweezers.

Mr Cole

The Headteacher was known to everyone as 'Miss Shoes', and it was only recently that I realized that her name must have been 'Miss Hughes'. My brother and I were evacuated from the South of England to a little village in Aberdeenshire, with children and teachers I did not know and to a completely different way of life. We stayed with kindly people but all I remember of my few months at the little village school was learning the 121st psalm by heart and an overwhelming feeling of homesickness.

I remember our needlework was dull. We knitted scarves for the army in khaki colour – it was quite an event when we moved on to air-force-blue socks. We were allowed to bring to school chocolate which we had bought out of our sweet ration. This we packed with the clothes we had made, compensating, I hope, for our bad knitting. Our days were enlivened by Shelter Practice and Gas Mask Drill.

Mrs Newman

Parents could contribute, too –

We all had free milk at morning break. It was placed on a back boiler so it was always warm to drink.

One boy named Alec Williams had great difficulty in pronouncing the letter 'h' and Miss Kidd (a real ogre) would make him stand in front of the whole class and recite, "He hit him on the head with a hard, hard, hammer". No matter how the poor boy tried he just could not do it.

Sue Maher

My own choice for telling stories from my school days was to use extracts from my school reports.

English – Peter finds it hard to write anything down. (6 yrs)
Maths – Peter is slow. It takes him twice as long as anyone else in the form to do a page of sums. (6 yrs)

A year later I was doing no better –

Cricket – Inclined to dream while fielding.
Class teacher's report – Peter is a dear little boy. He really is no trouble and always happy. But it is his nature to be slow.

When I was ten –

English – His writing as ever is poor.
Music – Peter tries hard – when he remembers.
Soccer – His kicking is weak.

Teachers and parents can collect memories in a scrapbook or duplicate them and turn them into a small booklet. These can act as triggers to children sharing stories of their earliest memories.

Quick ideas

Travelling story and news boards

There are many more opportunities than there used to be for meeting other teachers from local schools. This is a chance to create another audience for writing. Several schools join together and decide to send each other a news or story board. The boards have to be brought round on a certain day, and you need space to display them prominently. It is easier if schools are fairly close – perhaps some of the authors could travel with the boards to introduce themselves and the ideas they have explored. A plan for such an activity might run as follows.

a Each class decides on what it will put on to the boards. What will children in another school find interesting? Brainstorm some ideas. For example, jokes, where we live, stories, poems, news, recipes, questions, maps, photographs, cartoons, surveys, things we do in school, hobbies, how to make something.

b Individuals, pairs or groups decide on which elements they will write and present. Initial drafts will need to be shown back to the rest of the class to get a reaction. Is the content interesting, is it eye-catching, is it clearly displayed, should we use the wordprocessor?

c Final drafts are prepared. The boards (large sheets of thin card are suitable) are carefully mounted. Where are the spaces, how might they best be filled, would a tape recording go well with this?

Once you receive a board from another school, allow plenty of time for the children to read and react. An important part of the project is to encourage them to reflect on the content and presentation, and then to reconsider what they did! It is relatively simple to engage in a swap several times a year with local schools. This provides an increasing awareness that writing can communicate with an unknown audience, and that if it is to do so, you have to consider the interest level and presentation. It is interesting to invite children to jot down their initial reactions to the newsboard when it arrives.

> Some of it was hard to read because the writing was too small. I liked the jokes best. The photographs of the children were interesting.
>
> *Tina, 8 yrs*

Design a review

Groups could be asked to design their own review sheet. They will need to consider some sort of design to liven up the page, as well as headings or questions to direct the reviewer, for example

'How do you rate this story?' 'Would you recommend this to your best friend or worst enemy?' Successful sheets could be photocopied for class use. It should be remembered that the purpose of writing a review is to inform others about the book, so they can decide whether they would like to read it. A simple system could be established so that new books are reviewed and a copy of the review is placed in a scrapbook. Reviewers might be asked to make a brief presentation about the book to the rest of the class. Recommended reading might be displayed with the review sheet, beside a copy of the book.

The story hat

Start a collection of hats. Some could be designed and made by the children. When you sit with the children to read or tell a story, you wear the 'Story Hat'. Younger children will imitate the teacher quite happily and tell each other stories wearing the 'Story Hat'.

What sorts of stories might different hats tell? The hat could take you to different lands, it could turn you into someone else. Maybe it is a magic hat. What happens when you put it on? Small groups could take it in turns to work out a story for one of the hats, then make a presentation, telling the story to the rest of the class.

Cartoon time

Designing a cartoon to tell a well-known story is not such an easy task as it might appear. You have to decide which are the main images that tell the story, then try to summarise the story in a few words for each image without losing the excitement.

This exercise is best carried out in pairs. Each pair will need to draft out how many pictures are needed and what the content will be. If the cartoons are to be made into zigzag books, time will be needed to ensure the right wording, tidy presentation and neat handwriting. The wordprocessor may well be of assistance. The best cartoon booklets could be sent to another class and used as part of their reading material. If the books are taken home by other children, a brief introductory note might be useful – 'This book was written by Ros in Mrs Marsh's class'.

Pictures in the mind

After reading a story to the class, invite everyone to draw the part they remember the best. When they have drawn, put them in pairs to discuss why they chose that image, what they liked/ disliked about it, what it reminds them of. These images could be used in several ways.

a Take the drawings out in several days' time. Swap them round so that everyone has someone else's, and use them as the starting point to a new story.

b Take them out in a week's time and rewrite the story, making any changes you would like. Remind the children that stories are not fixed forever. We can change the fate and fortunes of the characters, set them in different places and times, introduce new problems and characters, and so on.

Stage three

Journeys in fiction

Rebecca's World by Terry Nation

Most children are fascinated by stories of happenings in other worlds. The world that Terry Nation creates for Rebecca is one that she finds herself in after looking through the wrong end of her father's telescope. She soon meets up with a bizarre trio – Grisby 'who has the most painful feet in the universe', Captain 'K' 'a reluctant and bespectacled superman', and Kovak 'an unemployed spy known as the man with a thousand faces – all of them embarrassingly alike'.

Rebecca soon learns that all is not well in her new world. With her three friends she sets out on an adventure to try to rid it of the evil ghosts that control it. Together they try to discover the last remaining ghost tree, as the wood from this tree exerts a strange power over the ghosts. Their attempts are hindered by the evil Mr Glister and his servants Lurk and Cringer, by a succession of strange creatures including the Swardlewardles who render their victims helpless by blowing laughing gas at them, and by the tongue twister monster who challenges Rebecca and her friends to invent a tongue twister that he cannot say.

Many children find *Rebecca's World* both amusing and exciting. Much discussion can take place about the main characters and their failings. How much of Kovak do we find in ourselves? Aren't we all chameleons to a certain extent, changing our appearances and attitudes to suit the situation? Mr Glister shows how easy it is to be lured by strangers with false smiles and plenty of money. Some children will enjoy making up imaginary conversations between Rebecca and her friends.

Others will be keen to find ways of helping Grisby to cure his foot trouble, or to concoct substances for Captain 'K' that might make him brave (in the same way that Popeye gains strength through spinach!).

Potion to cure bad feet

Take three drops of verruca cream, add corn plasters with a pinch of bunion powder and a squirt of foot cream. Mix it together and heat it up in a stained saucepan. It is called 'Footcure'.

Matthew James, 9 yrs

At one stage of the story Rebecca nearly falls prey to the 'Bad Habits'.

Potion for curing the Bad Habits

Take six bitten nails,
five sucked thumbs.
Ten chewed pens
and a bag of humbugs.
Mix them to make
'Habitcure'.

Julie Young, 9 yrs

There is great scope for dreaming up tongue twisters to test the power of the tongue twister monster. But beware too many contests, as some children may suffer the same fate as the tongue twister monster's servants, with 'their tongues curled like corkscrews'.

After reading *Rebecca's World*, children might enjoy inventing a world of their own or an imaginary planet. They could consider what it might be like in the legendary lands of Shangri-La, Tir-nan-Og, or Eldorado. Mollie Hunter writes of Tir-nan-Og at the conclusion of her novel *The Kelpie's Pearls* while Edgar Allan Poe's *Eldorado* and *Romance* by Walter James Turner tell us something of far-off lands that may or may not be reached.

Suggest that children name their world, give it continents, seas, cities, etc. They could then describe its size, shape, features, ruler, religions, houses, schools, clothes and people.

Maps and board games

Towards the conclusion of *Rebecca's World*, children might like to make a map of the journey that Rebecca and her friends accomplish before they discover the last ghost tree. A grid could be drawn on it, and coordinates plotted to show where the main events in the story took place – where Rebecca meets the Bad Habits, where Captain 'K' sews his tights together, where the splinter birds hatch out, and so on. Quizzes can also be devised to test mapping skills.

Making *Rebecca's World* board games can also prove popular, while at the same time showing children how necessary it is to write explicitly and carefully when giving instructions or directions. We remind them again and again of the need for accuracy in their writing, but unless we can give them reasons, that need will not be viewed as important.

One of the best ways to expose inaccuracies is to ask children, either working alone or in pairs, to design a board game (this can be as simple as a journey from A to B with hazards). Then they write out all the rules governing the game and the instructions for playing it. These should then be swapped with other children who try to play the game according to the rules and instructions they have been given.

Discussion can take place between the two parties, followed by subsequent modification, until an agreed set of rules and instructions are arrived at.

Any fictional account or real-life story that involves a journey of some kind is suitable for this purpose. Novels that may promote successful mapping and board-gaming are:

- *The Brothers Lionheart* – Astrid Lindgren
- *The House of Sixty Fathers* – Meindert Dejong
- The *Narnia* stories – C. S. Lewis
- *Journey of 1000 Miles* – Ian Strachan
- *I am David* – Anne Holm
- *Journey to Jo'burg* – Beverley Naidoo

The example opposite is a Spanish Armada board game incorporating elements of the game books that have become so popular in recent years.

As Matthew's fleet leaves Lisbon, you begin with 300 strength points. Red rings around a number mean trouble of some kind, while blue rings mean favourable winds to speed you on

KEY = ◎ A blue ring around a number means move on one space due to strong winds. (i.e. 18, 19, and 20)

KEY = ✳ Means smashed on rocks, deduct number of strength points as said above place number

KEY = ⬤ A red ring around a number means some kind of trouble If you land on number 12 or 13 go back to nine. If you land on 23 deduct 200. If you land on 28 or 29 deduct 50 strength points.

How to Play

Throw one dice if the number rolled is 1-3 move to spaces. If you throw 4-6 move 3 spaces.

The 'aim of the game' is to get back to Santander with as many fighting ships as you can.

START with 300 strength points.

START with 300 fighting ships when you leave Lisbon.

1 strength point = 1 fighting ship.

Go on to 15 if sent back to 9

MATTHEW PRINCE

Spanish Armada Game by Matthew Prince

85

your way. His instructions are clear. If you throw a 1 – 3 on
your dice, you move forward two spaces, a 4 – 6 means a
move of 3 spaces. Special numbers pose particular threats
where an appropriate number of strength points are forfeited.

Spanish Armada Game – *Matthew Prince, 9 yrs*

Diary-writing

When I first started teaching, the first half hour on a Monday
morning was taken up with the children writing in their news
books while I collected and counted dinner money. Many
children struggled with their writing. Had anything exciting
happened to them? No! Had they been anywhere interesting?
No! Had anyone visited them – Grandad or Grandma perhaps?
No!

One lad wrote the same thing in his notebook for five weeks in a
row: 'On Saturday I went shopping in Tescos, I pushed the
trolley, then we went home and had dinner. I played football
and then I watched 'Dr Who'. Then I had tea and went to bed'.

On the sixth week, after a lengthy session of 'Surely you did
something else at the weekend?', I was pleased to see the lad
writing furiously, and was eager to read what had prompted
this. Eventually he handed in two sides about his weekend visit
to … Australia! He told me everything, how he'd seen Sydney
Harbour bridge, the test match, koalas, kangaroos, etc.

It emerged after a while that he'd seen a TV programme about
Australia and was very keen to go there, so he did the next best
thing and let his imagination take flight!

It was a fine piece of work; he'd wanted to write on this
occasion, whereas he hadn't previously. After that I abandoned
weekly news writing!

There is, however, a place for diary-writing in the classroom
when the work is enjoyable for its own sake or linked to current
project activity.

Personal diaries

Children often find it valuable to have a book issued to them in which they can write what they like, and within reason, when they like. Such writing is then read by the teacher only if the child requests it. On some occasions such a book offers valuable therapy. I've seen children smouldering after a fight or a disagreement take out their writing journals, go back to their places and write furiously about what happened. Such writing can provide a period of catharsis for those involved.

Often, too, a poem or a piece of prose may emerge from something hastily scribbled down and then returned to at a later date. I encourage children to record things that they hear, one-liners that make them laugh, slogans, rhymes, etc.

Class diaries

The problem with personal diaries can be that after a while the initial flush of enthusiasm wears off. One way to avoid this is to initiate the keeping of a class diary. Those who wish to be involved (usually a high percentage of the class) find that they are only called upon to write in the diary once every four or five weeks. However, if the diary is maintained and built up into an attractive book, it can provide a fascinating record of all the major (and minor) achievements in one class during a school year.

Alternatively the diary could be sub-divided into
a events in class
b events in school
c national news, etc.

Project diaries

These are diaries that are kept for a short period of time and for a specific purpose, for example to record the growth of a sunflower from seed to flower, or to make observations on the progress of eggs in a classroom incubator.

Paul kept a diary in which he recorded changes in a swede that he'd sliced in half. He observed how it shrank, lost moisture and darkened in colour.

> **2/3/88** My swede has shrunk a lot now. For the first week it was very light in colour but now it has turned darker.

9/3/88 My vegetable has shrunk even more. It has got some lumps on it now and there's a big chunk out of it.

Paul Tiltman, 9 yrs

Diaries and fiction

Diary-writing can be used to help children empathise with the characters they meet in books.

In Beverley Naidoo's *Journey to Jo'burg*, Naledi and her brother Tiro travel three hundred miles from their village to the city of Johannesburg, so they can let their mother know that their baby sister Dineo is very ill.

In the city they experience apartheid at close quarters when they try to board a 'whites only' bus, and travel on crowded commuter trains.

At the end of each day, Naledi has learnt something new about her country and about herself.

This story works well with eight and nine-year-olds, and some interesting diary work can result from children looking at life in South Africa through Naledi's eyes. Remind children that they should write about how Naledi feels as well as about what has happened to her.

Anne Holm's *I am David* can be used as stimulus material in a similar way.

On another level entirely, Rebecca's nightly diary entries as she explores *Rebecca's World* with her three friends could make lively and entertaining reading. (See also examples of diary extracts in Section Five, p. 127.)

Fun diaries

There will be few children who are not familiar with the diary writings of Adrian Mole (alias Sue Townsend). Careful selected extracts could be read aloud and commented on. Think of how the diaries are written, i.e., Sue Townsend putting her thoughts into the head of fictitious Adrian Mole. Often children enjoy spending time on a similar idea. It is particularly useful towards the end of term, where some enthusiasm for writing has inevitably been lost and needs re-kindling.

Natasha puts herself in Santa's boots and although the following owes more than a passing nod to Raymond Briggs, it is nevertheless an entertaining read.

Santa's diary

23rd December

My wife and I were preparing for the long journey to all the houses. My suit has just been collected from the dry cleaners by my wife. I have been exercising the reindeer but Cupid wouldn't jump the hurdle. I had to fix the special hooves on the reindeer feet for flying. As it was colder than last year my wife said she would put a sheepskin rug in the sleigh. Then I waxed the bottom of my sleigh and made one of the elves polish the bridles.

24th December

I was in a state of panic. I was very upset because all the elves had colds so my wife and I had to wrap up the presents. I put the bridles on the reindeer and fixed the sleigh to the bridles. I got dressed into my red jacket, trousers, hat and black boots. I set off in the sleigh. I went down the first sooty chimney and got some soot in my mouth but I rinsed it out with a glass of sherry. When I had delivered all the presents I went home and had a peaceful sleep.

25th December

I woke up feeling happy with myself because I had delivered the presents in a faster time than usual. From my wife I had a new bobble hat. Tomorrow I plan to go on holiday to the South Pole.

Natasha Smith, 8 yrs

Ideas for prose writing

Advertisements

Newspapers are funded by advertisements, and it is both entertaining and illuminating to browse through the small ads and discover interesting items for sale. Many children enjoy composing an advertisement offering something for sale and extolling its virtues – or otherwise!

Brother for Sale

There's a brother for sale with
a world record for whining and complaining,
an everlasting chatter
and a helpful manner when sweets are about.
His Christmas list is always three and a half miles long.
He will eat all the scraps so keep him away from bins.
And all for 55p.
That's all I can afford.
Please take him away soon before I go crazy.

Tristan Towers, 8 yrs

Often this can be related to project work to give a 'fun' element to the study of a particular region, as in the example below:

Pyramid for Sale

Cheops & sons
An attractive semi-detached pyramid, full loft insulation and
gas central heating. Fully double glazed, complete with 50m
swimming pool, free video games and sauna.
1264 metres high with a good view over the Nile, and with
shops only two minutes walk away.
It should be a good buy for the first time buyer.
Mortgage available, only 4000 camels.

Edward Thomas, 9 yrs

Finally, what about advertising something for the sort of person who has everything already? Suggest that children think of a totally inessential product, but one which might serve some sort of purpose. In the example below, Adele is offering saucers that are especially made to be smashed:

Smashing Saucers

Saucers for the angry sort of person.
72 of these fabulous smashers.
Blue for the guys,
Pink for the girls.
Hurry along
It's a once in a lifetime bargain.
ON NOW
But only at B.A. Saucer Company.

Adele Tucker, 10 yrs

The fight

Most children have been in a fight at some time or other, and will be only too keen to relate their experiences.

You could begin by asking children to make a list of the most common causes of fights in school. Then ask them to write a few sentences trying to answer the main questions that we usually ask about a fight. Suggest that they write from experience if possible, and concentrate on how the fight started, who was involved, what happened, who won (if anyone), and what, if anything, was resolved?

Later these 'bare bones' of the incident can be fleshed out with a more detailed description that considers such factors as how those involved looked, what the atmosphere was like, the mood of the crowd (if appropriate), etc.

Alternatively a fight (as with any incident) could be reported from different angles and viewpoints. Children could write about the fight from the point of view of an adult who just happened to be passing, the policeman who broke it up, the kid sister of one of the fighters, or a sneak reporting the fight to his teacher.

Try writing two descriptions, one from the point of view of someone who supports you and the other from someone who supports your enemy. How would they differ?

The Fight

I arranged a fight with him during geography. It all started in lesson time when he pinched my ruler and engraved his name on it. Then he said it was his when the teacher asked whose it was.

I sat staring at his boasting friends as the bell went for the end of school. He went outside telling his friends how he would 'duff me up'. That was that, I stormed out of the classroom and snatched my belongings off the peg. Outside his ghastly friends looked at me, John, a big fat monster, Peter, a spotty youth, Tony, a small, stupid boy and him, John Daniels, a skinny staring fourth year. Oh why did I have to say that word FIGHT. Well after all he did take my ruler.

He stepped forward. I backed away without courage. Then I clenched my fists and dived at him. He showed his teeth as if he were a dog and bit my arm hard. Oh, it was agony. My

blood boiled inside. He grabbed at my throat and pressed my
neck against the cold wall. I felt sick and coughed,
desperately hoping he would let go, but he didn't, so I kicked
hard at him. He let go and grabbed his aching leg while I ran,
anywhere.

When I got home I thought to myself, how stupid! I have cuts
and bruises all over, I have made a fool of myself and it hasn't
solved the problem . . .
He's still got MY ruler!

Kerry Dale, 10 yrs

The Fight

It was a nasty winter's day and my sister and I were stuck
inside doing nothing. Then we started annoying each other for
nothing and calling each other silly things. As this is
happening I can feel anger building up inside me but try to
keep myself from hitting her. I just know she's going to hit me
in a minute so then I can hit her back. Then all at once I call
her a really silly name so she comes and hits me straight in
the stomach. This really makes me mad and I seem to erupt
like a volcano and start hitting her everywhere. Then she
starts crying and runs into the kitchen to tell on me. I just
stare at the door she went out and the erupting volcano
seems to turn into a cold lonely ocean with nothing solved
and nothing gained.

Spencer Sherwin, 9 yrs

Gulliver's pockets

Briefly relate the account of Gulliver's shipwreck and how upon
swimming ashore, he fell asleep, only to find when he woke that
he was the prisoner of tiny people no more than 15 cm high.

The tiny Lilliputians nicknamed him 'The Man Mountain', and
on the orders of the Emperor of Lilliput, a list was drawn up of
everything that was in Gulliver's pockets.

Below are two descriptions of items that were found. Children
may care to guess what they are:

*'One great piece of cloth, large enough to be a foot-cloth for your
Majesty's chief room of state.' '. . . a great silver chain with a
wonderful kind of engine at the bottom . . . fastened to that chain
appeared to be a globe, half silver and half of some transparent metal;
for on the transparent side we saw strange figures circularly*

drawn... He put this engine to our ears, which made an incessant noise like that of a water-mill; and we conjecture it is either some unknown animal or the god that he worships.'

There were other items on the list – Gulliver's snuff-box, comb, pistols, pocket-knife, razor, purse, money (gold pieces) and his sword.

Suggest that children write a short description of one of these items in the way that it might have been described on the Emperor's list. They can imagine that they are describing the object to someone who has no idea what it looks like or what it is used for.

Afterwards it can be fun to compare what the children have written with what Swift wrote in his book.

Now try this with other everyday objects. How would you describe a telephone to a caveman?

Look through your own pockets for something to describe.

Jump

Ask children to imagine themselves standing somewhere up high, with someone below or nearby yelling, 'Jump, just jump!'

Four possible situations:

a a high diving-board, when the next person waiting to dive has become impatient.

b a tall building on fire; the fireman's safety blanket is spread out below.

c your first parachute jump, when you feel reluctant to leave the plane.

d bird being taught how to fly, or a frog learning to jump.

There are many more possibilities. Suggest that children write a story that centres around an incident where the words 'Jump, just jump!' are used. The story might lead up to this or it could develop from it.

Recipes

A recipe is defined as a list of ingredients and instructions for making something, often a food dish.

Children can have fun making up recipes in all kinds of situations. When challenged to concoct something that might satisfy a dragon's hunger pangs, Stephen cooked up –

Blood Nasties

Blood nasties are lovely snacks.
Here are the ingredients.

1kg snakes' eyes,
10 pints of blood,
80 eggs,
18 pints of poison.

First put all the ingredients in a bowl and make a squelchy mixture. Then take it to Death Valley to cook. Leave it for 20 minutes then go and get it.

Stephen Buss, 9 yrs

In the example below, Imogen stirs up a birthday mix for her wordprocessor.

2 boiled 'buts',
3 fried 'ands',
20 jellied 'ifs'.

Put it in the oven
(and over bake it)
Make sure it is black and smells of 'whens' when it comes out.

Icing

Beat 10 'ats' (if they scream so much the better)
Pour it into a bowl and put it in the fridge.
Then put it on the cake 20 minutes afterwards.

Warning!

Feed it to your wordprocessor, not to yourself.

Imogen Hibbert, 8 yrs

Most children will be familiar with the old rhyme that answers the question, 'What are little boys (and little girls) made of?'

This idea may be extended to family members and friends. Think of all the things that remind you of the person you are writing about. Make a list if you like, then include them in a recipe.

Granny Recipe

My granny is made of a bar of smooth sweet chocolate, a heart of glittering gold and old socks with holes in.

My granny is made of a patchwork cushion, a box of cotton wool and knitting needles working together.

My granny is made of a bottle of kindness and love, a bunch of primroses and a mug of steaming hot coffee.

My granny is made of curly grey hair, a pair of gold rimmed spectacles and a mind of knowledge and stories.

My granny is made of an old fashioned lamp glowing red and yellow, an old fashioned shawl and happy laughter.

Natasha Smith, 10 yrs

Dream jars

At the start of Roald Dahl's *The BFG*, Sophie is watching out of her window at night when she sees something that certainly isn't human. It is 'Something very tall and very black and very thin.'

She sees the giant figure empty the contents of a jar into the mouth of a trumpet and then blow through it into the upstairs room of a house.

Later Sophie discovers that the giant is blowing dreams into children's bedrooms.

'Dreams,' he said, 'is very mysterious things. They is floating around in the air like little wispy misty bubbles.'

'Every morning I is going out and snitching new dreams to put in my bottles.'

Sophie enjoys reading the labels that the BFG writes for his dream jars. Usually they are descriptions of the kind of dream that the jar contains. Some of the descriptions are quite long, and stretch right round the jar.

It is a good idea to read one of the BFG's labels before the children begin to write. Mention may be made of the BFG's bad spelling, and a decision taken as to whether this will be acceptable from children in this instance.

Tell the class that the BFG has collected too many dreams, and needs help with writing labels. Here are some suggestions for dreams that require labels.

- A dream involving horses and a member of the Royal Family.

- A dream about beings from another planet and a first division football match.

- A dream about a baby brother or sister and water from an overflowing bath cascading down the stairs.

- A dream involving a strict teacher and a baby dragon that hatches from an egg.

- A dream of knights in armour and rescuing a damsel in distress from the 21st floor of a tower block.

The collaborative story

Many professional writers are quite happy working alone. Others enjoy meeting with fellow writers to exchange views and discuss ideas.

This is also true of young writers in school. Some hate the idea of anyone else having a say in what they write, while others enjoy the chance to discuss and to seek reassurance. Sometimes successful collaborations can take place in the writing of a book. Two children working together can try out ideas on each other before committing them to paper. They can also take turns with writing out the book neatly and illustrating it.

Group writing can be a valuable activity when there are clear-cut parts for each member to play in the story. In one project on 'Giants', my children were developing their ideas about a 'Giants' Olympics'. Each child had invented his or her own giant and had taken it through a number of preliminary stages until the day of the actual Olympic contest.

Discussion then took place over how the contest would develop, with each group member deciding what part his or her giant would play in the event, i.e., who would win, who would cheat, who would start a fight, etc.

Some children continued working in groups and developed their Giants' Olympics into an adventure on the lines of 'fighting fantasies' or 'choose your own adventure' stories. They used their giant's journey home from the Olympics as the basis of the story.

The school of the future

Already there are schools in the USA where children are taught by a robot for part of the day. In San Francisco, three classes of thirty pupils in neighbouring schools are taught simultaneously by 'Big Brother'.

Could it happen here?

Children will be only too eager to tune into their own visions of the future.

> There will be small lights on the ceiling which are really force-fields to keep you in your desk.
>
> All the classrooms will be bugged so that the head-robot can hear all the school and tell them off. There will be a screen where he can put up all the work for the week.
>
> Robo Teacher 1, RT1 for short, is the world's first robot teacher. It took 15 years to build, mainly from 6R2-71-B silicon chips in BS R15 plastic with gold and copper terminals. The power box is an iron box coated with TP162 plastic. It can teach anything. Here are a few of the programs: Paint 1, Art 1, Art 2, Art 3, English (full-stops) and Maths (long multiplication).
>
> The work goes in RT1's input slot, RT1 marks it and it comes out of the 'out' slot. RT1 has 40 joints, 17 in the legs, 14 in the arms, 5 in his body and 3 in his head. He has a microprocessor card in his head too.
>
> When you buy one, you get a 1000 mark pack but you can buy extra ones. The prices are from £825 for a 2000 mk pack to £40,000 for a 50,00 mk pack. You can also buy word banks starting with a 500 word bank.
>
> *Edward Thomas, 10 yrs*

Lists

Most children enjoy itemising their likes or dislikes, for example 'five things I love/hate about being a child', or 'five meals I absolutely love/loathe', etc. Other kinds of lists can stretch their imaginations and their resourcefulness – 'ten items I'd need to help me survive on a desert island', for example.

Some lists can simply be fun to work on as time-fillers or end-of-term activities. Ask children to think of five or ten disasters that might befall someone or something!

10 Disasters for Children

1 Missing your favourite TV programme to find something out for your teacher.

2 Waking up and finding out it's a school day.

3 When the dog has just licked your face or dribbled down your leg.

4 Cleaning out your pet's hutch.

5 When your little brother or sister has just pulled the head off your doll or action man and you're watching it sink in the bath.

6 Hymn practice.

7 When Dad's told you that you can't watch 'EastEnders' because he's going to watch a cowboy and indian film.

8 When Mum's gone out, your big sister's at work, your little sister's screaming at you and you're doing the washing up.

9 Wrapping up presents and getting tape stuck over you.

10 Peeling hard boiled eggs.

Kellie Penfold, 9 yrs

5 Disasters for Superman

1 His tights are in the wash.

2 The colour in his boxer shorts washes out and they're now pink.

3 He forgets to switch on the lights in his eyes.

4 His Dad tells him not to start fights.

5 His Mum says to be in by 8.00 and in bed by 9.00.

Matthew Prince, 9 yrs

Children love to be invited to joke in this way, and more often than not it is the technically less proficient writers who come up with the most amusing ideas.

Metamorphosis

'As Gregor Samsa awoke one morning from uneasy dreams he found himself transformed in his bed into a gigantic insect.'

Thus begins *Metamorphosis*, a short story written by the Austrian author Franz Kafka. Samsa discovers that he has been changed into a giant beetle. The sheets and blankets slide off him easily enough, but there are other, seemingly insurmountable difficulties to overcome – how to get off his back and out of bed, how to open the bedroom door, how to get downstairs and how to communicate with his family and friends.

Children enjoy this bizarre situation and will readily offer all kinds of ingenious ideas as to how Gregor can overcome his problems. They may also enjoy putting themselves in his place and writing about their changeover to some insect or creature.

I just managed to raise my head and saw instead of my usually skinny body, I had an ant's!! Oh well, I said, ant or no ant I'll have to get out of bed. I tried rolling from one side to the other but that didn't work. Then I had a brain-wave. I raised my abdomen and brought it crashing down on the bed. In doing so I was raised at the top of my abdomen. I couldn't balance and fell flat on my face . . .

Robert Thompson, 10 yrs

With this idea I always insist that the story should not finish with the line 'It was all a dream ...'!

Another excellent starting point comes from *Bill's New Frock* by Anne Fine: *'When Bill Simpson woke up on Monday morning, he found he was a girl.'*

Quick ideas

Supermums and supergrans

All mums, dads, grans and grandads are special in some way. Ask children to choose a family member and invest him or her with super powers:

'My supermum spends money like lightning. She tidies rooms and cleans in two minutes. She drives a car like a torpedo. She can cook anything, if she's got a cook book.

My gran has got rocket boosters under her long-johns so she can make it to tea.'

Letter to an alien

E.T. seems to have been responsible for unleashing upon us a whole rash of friendly aliens in recent years. It is now just as likely, when the little green men appear, for children to tell their troubles to an alien agony aunt, rather than to alert the cops and then hide under the bed!

Suggest that children compose a letter to an alien who has recently visited them, describing the effect that the visit had on the household and the local community.

Directions from my house to school

Either with the aid of a street plan or from memory, give directions to someone who is unfamiliar with your locality. Take care to give correct instructions as to where to turn left or right, and indicate local landmarks on the journey.

Draw a map if it makes things easier. Take the directions home with you and try to follow them next morning to check their accuracy. Re-write with modifications if necessary.

A place for a story

Think of somewhere you know which might provide the setting for a story. Use a paragraph to describe the place and say what kind of story might be set there. Suggest characters and a brief outline of a possible plot. Write the story if you wish.

£5 notes floated from an upstairs window

Who? Where? Why? Sketch in a background and compose a story either beginning with this incident or leading up to it.

Stage four

The Mustang Machine

Chris Powling's *The Mustang Machine* is an exciting story about two rival gangs, which culminates in a biking contest between the leaders. The 'mustang machine' is a bike that is alive, that moves of its own accord ... the question is, can it be tamed to use in the contest?

The idea for the book began when Chris Powling asked his class what they would like for Christmas. One lad said a bicycle – not an ordinary bicycle, but one that was alive, like a mustang.

The book explores a number of different themes to do with leadership, bullying, anger, friendship and fair play. What price does a good leader have to pay?

The book is excellent for classroom use – not only because the story has a fast pace, confronts genuine dilemmas that concern children, connects with their lives and leads excitingly on to the end, but also because it centres around bicycles which hold an interest and importance for many children. A bike means freedom.

As the reading of the story progresses, a body of work can be built around the themes within the story and around the topic of bicycles.

A topic on bicycles

Pencil drawings of parts of a bicycle or the whole frame can be worked on. Push back the tables to create space in the room for several bikes to be positioned. Drawings from close observation can be developed through simple printing of bike shapes using polystyrene tiles, making prints of mechanical shapes, making model bikes with straws or balsa wood, or using circles to design patterns.

Once the children have completed close observation drawings of a bike, they could move into writing descriptions. An easy way into this is to jot down words, phrases and ideas as you stare at the bike and then build around these.

The wheels spin like a ballerina pirouetting. The black seat gleams in the sunlight like the jaw of a crocodile. The huge pump sits like a truncheon on a policeman's bike. The handlebars are shaped like ram's horns. The jewelled pedals have long strips of light. The reflector shines like a giant coin as the sun gleams. The spokes stream in different directions like a spider's web spun.

The history of bicycles from the 'Hobbyhorse', 'Boneshaker' and the 'Penny Farthing' to the tricycle and tandem and finally the BMX, not only reveals a variety of structures but also provides opportunities for looking at design and technological aspects of wheels, steering, cogs, brakes, friction, etc.

Local bike shops may provide brochures to study. Groups could design their own modern bike, with the accompanying brochure and poster to sell it. Perhaps the challenge could be to design a bike for a specific purpose – a policeman's bike, an elephant's bike ...

The theme of safe bicycling can lead into looking at protective and sensible clothing, how to ride correctly, road signals and signs. Signs can be designed and tested for clarity in the playground. The local road-safety officer could be invited to give a relevant introduction to road safety. Of course, the ideal time for such a project would be when the school road-safety tests are being carried out. This may lead into planning a day's bicycling route using local maps. Where would you like to visit? Which roads would be best to use and why? How far could you travel comfortably and how long might it take? The last question may lead children into suggesting and trying out ways of calculating how quickly you travel on a bike. What would you take with you on your day's outing? List the contents of the bicyclist's perfect knapsack.

Most people like to travel quickly on bicycles, but it's fun to have a slow bike race where the winner is the last to the line. This could lead on to movement work on balance as well as a closer look at ways of slowing down, using brakes and friction. Labelled diagrams of the relevant parts of the bike, so the children learn the appropriate terminology, are useful. Where possible children should be able to design and test their own simple tricycles that use some form of simple braking system.

A school survey – with the results published on a general display board for all to see – could explore such questions as 'How many people own a bike?' 'What age groups use a bike?' 'What is the main use – coming to school or recreation?'

Ask the children to write one chapter only from a story in which someone is being pursued and in order to escape, leaps on a bicycle. Giving these confines means that the children's focus will be more on the quality of description and less on the plot.

> The bike had been left against the bridge. There was no one now in sight. He knew that it was his only chance. He steered the bike away from the bridge. He jumped on to the saddle making the spring squeak. He kicked up the stand and pushed up with his feet. Before him lay a hill sloping steeply down, so he flicked the gear lever up into third gear. It was a bleak day, the sun had just about managed to poke through the low cloud one or two times. There was quite a strong wind, it stung his face. At the bottom of the hill was an alley, he cut through it to take a short cut. The wheels made a crackling noise on the loose gravel . . .
>
> *Adrian Morris, 9 yrs*

Exploring themes from the story

The story of *The Mustang Machine* lends itself to much extension work, exploring many of the issues confronted. It is an ideal book to use as a build up to drama sessions, exploring the themes of anger and dominance.

In pairs – one a bully, one a coward – explore through movement and mime a position which shows the relationship between the two. Then swop over so that the coward becomes the dominant person. Now discuss how the different roles felt. This could move on to silent miming of anger. Pretend that you are angry, shout and show your anger in silence. In a circle, you could begin with one child who is angry. Bring into the circle someone else who has to help diffuse the situation. Try choosing a child who finds it hard to control her temper to do the calming down. What sorts of things make us angry? How do we feel? What do we do when someone is angry?

Sitting in a circle, mime a box in front of you. When you are selected, you open your box and some anger or frustration comes out. Someone else in the circle is chosen to help you out of it. When you have calmed down, the box lid is closed, signalling the end of the improvisation. This explorative work on anger could come just after Becca's explosion at the end of the second chapter.

The story lends itself to illustration – especially of the bike flying – as well as writing new stories about the mustang machine. Supposing you found the bike – where might it take you? What if your dad found it and thought you had stolen it?

There are a number of key moments within the story. It could be that these parts are read and enjoyed with no further comment. However, judging the mood of the class, you may wish to provide activities that take the children closer to the heart of the story's themes. Here are some suggestions from a planned topic on the theme of the book, used with a class of thirty village school children, aged seven to eleven years.

Chapter one. In groups, one person is selected to be interviewed.That person has to pretend that she has seen the mustang machine. The others are reporters for local papers. Tape your interview for the other groups to listen to.

Chapter two. Jot down in your notebook what you think might be wrong with Tim. What sorts of qualities do you need to have, to be a leader? In your group draw up a list to present to the class. How do you think the children feel when they are called 'little wogs' by Dennis? Discuss in your group how you should react to people making such comments. How could you help to change their minds? Why might people say things like that?

Chapter five. In your group, list down different reasons why people might become bullies. Do you think that bullies want to be liked? What does Tim mean when he says, 'The trouble is when he behaves like that they hate him even more which makes him feel even uglier. It's a kind of vicious circle.'?

Chapter six. How would you capture the bike? Draw up a plan of action and be ready to present your ideas to the class. You may use sugar paper, felt-tips, etc to draw diagrams if need be.

Chapter eleven. If Becca wins the contest, they hope that Dennis will change. What does your group think will happen? Prepare an account of the end of the book to present to the class.

Chapter thirteen. Hold a class debate to discuss whether it is right for Becca to enter the contest, or whether it is cheating.

Chapter fifteen. Mime a scene in which someone is getting really angry and someone gives the wrong reaction – laughs, yawns, or seems very pleased.

End of the story. How did you feel about Dennis? What might happen to Tim? Write the next chapter.

You are a reporter and have seen the final challenge with Tim and Dennis. Write a report for the local paper.

Journey to Boravia

This idea leans on the current interest in creating new myths, as well as the popular trend in 'adventure' books, where an option is given and the reader determines how the adventure might go. It is, in essence, an idea that borrows from the tradition of 'the quest'.

A basic outline can be given to the class, such as:

A group of travellers are to journey from SELINOS to BORAVIA carrying with them the precious stone, 'the eye of the world'. The dying king of Boravia must have the stone for it has great healing powers. His physicians believe that only the stone can save him. In order to reach Boravia, dangerous lands must be crossed.

Each child decides on their companions, draws them and writes a brief description outlining their abilities.

A map showing where the adventure takes place could be designed, but is best drawn once the adventure is complete.

The teacher outlines the starting point then gives a number of options for each child to choose from. Each child could select their option by throwing dice, drawing straws or pulling a card, rather than by making a free choice, if you wish.

So, chapter one could begin with the group of travellers being given the stone by the great magician Hawk. As they leave the palace, one of the following options occurs:

- It starts to collapse.
- They are attacked by wolves.
- They fall into a deep pit.

Each child decides which challenge to meet, and writes their first chapter explaining what happens and how they escape from the palace.

The second chapter begins with the travellers leaving the palace gates behind them and travelling through the great wood. Once again, a series of options can be suggested. For example:

- The trees come alive.
- They find themselves in a wood of utter darkness.
- Trolls steal their horses.

By the end of the second chapter they are leaving the other side of the wood.

The pattern might continue like this:

Chapter 3 – Crossing a lake.
- A monster upsets the boat.
- The lake freezes over.
- A serpent offers them a lift.

Chapter 4 – Travelling through the town of Dartsam.
- They are seized by soldiers.
- One of the group gets lost.
- The stone is stolen by a pickpocket.

Chapter 5 – Hiding from a storm in a cave.
- A bear comes in.
- The cave is blocked by a landslide.
- The cave leads to a chamber full of strange lights.

Chapter 6 – Crossing the mountains.
- Chased by a dragon.
- Attacked by flying dogs.
- Pursued by snakes.

If you are to provide the whole class with similar options, the children need to know where they should make each chapter end. There are other ways to organise such a project – the most successful being a group writing project. The group should determine the characters and plot before beginning, and allocate tasks which may go on to include illustration, contents page, notes on contributors, publicity blurb, etc.

This sort of project demands time. It may take as long as a term. Ongoing work should be stored in a folder. There will need to be plenty of time for children to read their work in progress to each other as well as to the teacher. The complete story should be made into a book which can be used in the class library. Once the children have seen how to construct this kind of story, they may be ready to write their own quest. Try reading one for the class story.

Good stories to read as a lead into this sort of extended work include:

- *The Hobbit* – J.R.R. Tolkien
- *Erik the Viking* – Terry Jones
- The *Narnia* series – C.S. Lewis
- *The Phantom Tolbooth* – Norton Juster
- *The Brothers Lionheart* – Astrid Lindgren
- *The Dark is Rising* – Susan Cooper

After reading *Erik the Viking*, Anna began her own extended book project on a Viking saga. She began with what she called 'Book Details'.

Name of Viking warrior: Bjorn the Brave.

Name for his ship: The Sly Sea Serpent.

Bjorn the Brave and his men are on a journey to find adventure. The sea monster has 3 magical powers. One, if you look into its eyes they will dazzle you. Two, its skin is so tough and thick that no sword can even scratch it and three, it is so large that it can swallow ships whole. The only way that it can be killed is by blinding it. Bjorn the Brave is a good leader because he is very brave. He is good at steering the ship, using his sword and deciding.

Her story begins:

'I've chosen you Sven', said Bjorn the Brave. 'Here's a knuckle bone. And last but not least' Bjorn said 'Here's a knuckle bone for you Tom. Now that I've chosen everyone for the voyage to find new lands and we've built the ship lets go!' Bjorn's men cheered and slapped each other on the back. They said goodbye to their wives and children and then waded out to their ship, The Sly Sea Serpent, and took up their oars and rowed.

As part of the story Anna includes a spell, a test and a poem:

A spell for protection against evil

Journey to the silver moon on a glittering star where you will find a unicorn. Steal its horn and hollow it out. Blow seven times through the horn and the old man of the moon will give you a thin whisp of his long, flowing beard. Travel to the bright, burning sun on a fierce eagle, pluck a feather from its left wing in exchange for the whisp of beard then fling the feather into space. Collect three red rose petals and take them to the edge of the world where an old silver oak tree waits. Place one petal in its branches, the second petal at its roots and the third petal inside the trunk. In this way you will be protected from evil.

Three ways to test a Viking's strength

He must be able to slay a sea monster, split a boulder in two with a sword and he must be able to walk across fire.

At the edge of the world

At the edge of the world I saw
a golden swan swim a lake of silver shining water,
a book that ate words,
a glittering spider's web covered in jewels,
an eagle with fluffy wings of snowflakes,
a unicorn with a mane of foam,
a tiny seed that would eventually grow
into another planet the size of the world,
a shiny, pearl-white dragon's tooth
and a waterfall that ran into an ocean.

The book was illustrated and included factual details that she had researched about the Vikings as well as designs for shields, carved posts, helmets and swords. There was a map, a Viking word search and details about the author and her previous publications. The story contains many traditional elements – monsters, enchantments, etc. A terrible storm nearly wrecks the boat, but the Vikings survive. When they find land they set off to explore ...

> Bjorn was walking through the trees when he heard a soft voice singing a beautiful tune. He wanted to see whose lovely voice he was listening to so he moved towards the tune. Soon he came to a cave where the tune seemed to be coming from so he stepped inside feeling quite tired and drowsy. The voice seemed even more beautiful than when he had first heard it so he walked on and on through the cave feeling sleepier and sleepier. Now that he had gone a long way he could no longer see the entrance or where he was going. The voice was like a lullaby and Bjorn was just about to drop off to sleep when ahead of him he could see a warm, bright light. Bjorn longed to go to sleep but he also longed to get to the light where he guessed the lovely voice was coming from. He moved closer and closer to the light and got a shock when he could see where the voice was coming from. A green creature about the size of Bjorn was singing. The creature was slimy and had spikes all over its body. It had thin slits for its eyes and its tongue was long and green. The song went on and on as if it were telling Bjorn to close his eyes and sleep. He curled up on the cold, stony floor and slept.

Bjorn's crewmates free him, they discover treasure, defeat the sea monster and finally reach home.

Anna's main characters were all male. Stereotyped views can be challenged through such stories as *The Practical Princess* by Jay Williams or *Bill's New Frock* by Anne Fine.

Ideas for prose writing

Using postcards

A large collection of postcards, photographs and other images can act as a useful starting point for writing. Images of people and places, as well as postcards of paintings, can be gathered easily over a period of time. These could be used in a variety of different ways. It is important to provide a broad selection – at least fifty images – and a variety. The traditional pretty postcard does not act as an exciting trigger to memory, nor does it evoke much response. Children are more excited by images that intrigue, that are bizarre, that ask questions, that seem to hold a story. Try to provide images that might either evoke a memory or stimulate a desire to re-create the image in words, or act as an intriguing element in a story.

The ability of the surrealists – Dali and Magritte in particular – to excite with a bizarre sense of fun, appeals greatly to children. To children nothing is fixed – the fierce potency of their imagination allows for anything to happen. The surrealists' world is close to a child's own sense of excitement and fun.

The collection of cards might be used in any of the following ways. Begin by laying out all the cards, so there is a wide choice of images. Let the children choose an image that appeals.

a What does the picture remind you of? Write about a memory associated with it. What happened? Where were you? Take yourself back there. What do you feel? Why was the memory important? Take us back there. What can you see? What can you hear?

b Pretend that the picture is an illustration in a story. Write the page facing it. By doing this, the writer is free to concentrate on the quality of the writing; the focus is not taken up by a concern for plot. It tends to cut out 'and then ... and then ... and then ...'

c Use the picture as a starting point for a descriptive poem. Select details and describe them. Give each detail a separate sentence or line. Perhaps begin by jotting down, very quickly, any first impressions, thoughts, words or ideas. Take some of these and flesh them out.

d Write a letter to an imaginary friend. Use the postcard as the starting point for the content of the letter.

e Choose a postcard of a famous place. Using reference books, write a holiday brochure.

f Choose a card and write the advertising slogan that goes with it.

g Pretend that the picture you have chosen is the front cover of a book – now write the story that goes with it.

The coal miner

His blacked out face matches the pitch black wall. His rigid chin is like the humps that a camel would have. His long neck juts up with strength and authority. His old torn sweater is smothered in dust and smudged by splinters of coal. His stern face glares at the dark passage to nowhere.

Nico Van der Wurf, 8 yrs

Hell's emblem

The devil's arms reach out pulling you closer, closer, until you perish in his heat. The shield with its burning eye looks, following you around, its bloody tears sweeping everything in their path. The knight's head, its tongue as quick and as painful as a whip possessed by Indiana Jones. The head, a ruby glittering in the flames of the devil, still grasps you closer. The two creatures clutch the shield with two hands or hooves. The horse, its hind legs a mass of roots, the baboon's teeth are as sharp as a hunting knife.

Paul Rock, 10 yrs

The silver dollar bar

Cigarette ends stubbed out on the silver ashtray. Money handed over for a pint – beer, lager or a vodka. You name it, its there. The choked smell of cigars and cigarettes feels as if it is a tarry smokebox. Gloomy faces stare, a world of aliens, not knowing where they are. The drunks laugh at even the sickest jokes. The smell of stale booze is sickly too. Coffee spilt onto the clean floor. The nag, nag, nag of the caretaker, for even he is a beer spiller. The dumpy waiters wander round with menus of no variety, just fish and chips. Stammering around, some drinkers are driving. The flat top of the barman with the skinhead cut and the dollars handed over. Adverts on the wall, not an unusual sight but one or two people take notice. The silver dollars are a common sight. They are payment for drowsiness.

Ralph Wood, 9 yrs

Christmas ideas

At Christmas-time, classrooms are full of children busily writing notes to Santa and cards for friends, to post in the school letterbox, making endless mobiles of snowflakes, and spending a lot of time colouring in and waiting around for the school play to begin! More imaginative writing ideas could include

a Magical gifts – a necklace made of fire, a teddy-bear made of sunsets, a book made of disasters, a new pair of shoes made of sneezes ...

b Father Christmas's diary.

> **23rd December.** Got up early to finish wrapping presents, helped wife make some mince pies. Emptied the potato sacks and filled them with the presents.
>
> **24th December.** Put on my red suit (could hardly do the buttons up) and bridled the reindeer, polished their antlers. Got stuck in the second chimney I visited but the reindeer helped me through. When I came out I almost slid off the roof but my faithful reindeers stopped me. They could probably smell the sherry I'd drunk and wanted some! After that I shared my mince pies with them. Arrived home later than last year, my wife said I was drunk! Went to bed with my boots on ...
>
> **25th December.** Didn't get up till lunch time, pulled two crackers and got a purple party hat and a miniature plastic Father Christmas, looked nothing like me ...
>
> *Anna Budd, 9 yrs*

c Write a story in which Father Christmas gets into trouble:

> One day on Christmas Eve Father Christmas was loading up a sack when there was a yell from number 24 on the calendar. He got a shock when number 6 sprang in 24's place. He said, 'Dear, dear, it must not be time to go yet.' He stared at it and then said, 'Well I'll start to unload my sack, I'm sure it was the 24th'. Just then the police came round and said, 'Why aren't you going out?' 'Because, its the 6th', said Father Christmas. The police looked at each other and stared and stared at the calendar ...
>
> *Matthew Cole, 7 yrs*

d Rewrite the bible story in a modern idiom.

> Once upon a time there was a lady called Mary. She was engaged to a fellow called Joseph. One day when she was doing the housework an unusual person rang the bell ...
>
> *Alison Bunney, 7 yrs*

e About a month before the end of the Christmas term, ask a

113

parent to dress up as Father Christmas and make a surprise visit – children could interview the visitor and later write letters.

> Dear Father Christmas. Thank you for coming to see us and thank you for answering our questions and thank you for giving up your time to come and see us. I liked the way you were being funny and thankyou for letting Mrs Jackson tape for us and I hope you come and see me some time and I will leave you some pie and drink.
>
> Love from Karen.
>
> *Karen, 6 yrs*

Other festivals can also be celebrated through story. Divali, for instance, should be a time when the tale of Rama and Sita is told.

On the buses

Ask the children to describe a journey by bus. Who is on the bus, where do you go, what do you see as you travel along, what are people talking about?

A good way to introduce this lesson is through drama. Arrange seats as if you were on a bus, and begin to introduce characters on to and off the bus. You will need a conductor. Children can decide who they will be beforehand. An interesting way to do this is by using 'newspaper faces'. Cut out a selection of faces from the papers. Everyone taking part chooses a face and decides what that person is like – their name, age, occupation, family, interests, etc. Another way to add to the improvisation is to give each participant an envelope with brief details about a character and their concern, for example: 'Young mum worried about being late for an appointment at the clinic'.

> I clamber up the winding staircase hesitating and muttering to myself. I hear the heavy doors squeal shut. I am flung back into a demolished seat and see graffiti on the back of the seat. I close my eyes and twiddle my thumbs from place to place. The blinding sun makes a cascade of a cluster of colour. The sweat oozes out of my pores. I hear someone muttering a joke, very quietly. I take no notice of my mind, I just chuckle away to myself. A lady with a dog catches my eye. The lady has a bright pink shirt which doesn't go well with her at all.

Finally my bus screeches to a halt then my journey is ended
at last.

Richard Cobbold, 9 yrs

A true bus stop story

Sitting at the bus stop I was bored and fed up. It was raining,
not hard, just a drizzle. An old lady walked up to me. Her eyes
twitching and her mouth moving but producing no sound. She
sat down beside me and took a paper bag out of her pocket.
She offered me what was in it. I looked. They were just old
bits of paper. I shook my head. She looked different now, the
happy expression faded into an unhappy look. She offered
once more and I couldn't refuse. I took a piece of paper and
said thank you. The old woman smiled now and she made me
realize that I was lucky and I too began to smile.

Helen Quaintmere, 12 yrs

The book of flies

Everybody designs a flying creature and all the drawings go into
an *Observers' Book of Flies*, accompanied by the relevant details.
To introduce the idea you will need to read extracts from
appropriate books so the children know the sorts of headings
and language required: habitat, feeding, lifespan, etc.

Red-Backed Fly

So named because of the red stripes on its back. Flys
between April and July. Eggs are seven and found
underneath cars. Young found in sewers. It has scent glands
on its head that give a pungent smell when alarmed.

Nancy Bray, 9 yrs

The large-winged bird-eating fly

This fly is the largest specimen of the bird-eating flies. The
male has a small sting at the bottom of his abdomen which
enables him to poison the bird. They lay over a thousand
young but only about five survive. The female grows so heavy
when she is pregnant that she can't fly and that is why the
male makes the nest. Their legs are so powerful that they can
carry a fully grown eagle. They live in small areas of the
mountains.

William Foord, 9 yrs

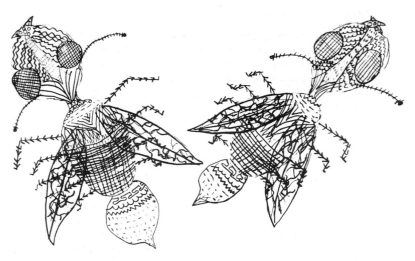

Flies by Coral Jeffrey

Memorable characters

Encourage children to describe someone they know, or to build up a character using a combination of different people. Get them to focus on the details – clothing, height, hair colour, sound of voice, typical things they say, how they walk. Children should be encouraged to use their notebooks to jot down observations of people they have seen, recalling what it was that was distinctive or memorable. People are brought alive by the small details.

This lesson links well with improvising different situations involving various characters. A useful starting point is to focus on writing about 'a friend', then move on to a member of the family. Older children respond well to writing about 'The most memorable person that I've met'.

Grandad

My grandad is fat with his braces almost breaking. Huge man with a skinny wife. Who live in a small house which is a squeeze. He collects stamps of all kinds. He was in the second world war and used to show where the pilots had to go. Once his plane crashed in a field but none of them were hurt. His wife is kind and always giving sweets.

Simon Overbury, 9 yrs

Ian

The last of the Teddy boys. Hair greased and slicked into a cool D. A. Drape jacket, blue suede shoes, drainpipes. Hail Rock and Roll. Bop to the music, but the last of the Teddy Boys dances alone. No bobby-soxer, no ... girl. No girl in the black stockings and bobby sox. No girl in the petticoats swirling.

Lisa Bowley, 13 yrs

I watched her unhurried movements, time is not relevant to her. Her shrivelled skin stretches over her sharp bones, leaving a pocket of skin sagging under her chin. She clutches the edge of the seat for support as she shakily sinks into the cushioned seat. Her withered face, weary. The narrow hand clutched the ragged shopping bag – then swift as a cat, it rose to her face, wiping away the spittle which was trickling down her stubbled chin. She sunk into the depths of her overcoat and appeared to drift off into sleep. The bus jolted, the old lady slipped, her mouth opened as if to cry out. No sound came. She could not speak.

Maria Stanford, 14 yrs

Portrait by Boyd Necker

Transposition stories

In these stories, the writer takes a character he already knows, and invents a new story and setting. This might be a matter of putting Little Red Riding-Hood into a new story in which she runs a corner shop, or of rewriting the original story with some changes. For instance, Cinderella's coach takes the wrong turning and she ends up at the Kebab house. A good game to play with younger children is to tell them a popular tale in which you have changed a number of important details. As you tell the story, the audience has to spot the 'mistakes'. They score a point for each change spotted, and the story-teller scores a point for each change that no one spots. Older children could write their own versions to try out with younger classes, once you have played the game several times.

You Only Live Once!

Story so far:
Code name 001 and a half, known as James Pond, licence to kill. Mission – collect data about nuclear attack plans on England from Russia. Whilst trying to collect a computer disc from a barman, Pond has been involved in a fight, been knocked unconscious and slung in prison.

Pond scanned the concrete cell through his bloodshot eyes. The steel entrance steadily opened, revealing a frowning man, accompanied by two muscular guards. He introduced himself as Major Shikofski . . .

Boyd Necker, 10 yrs

Clever Polly and the Stupid Wolf by Catherine Storr is a good example of a well-known tale with some changes made.

Superpowers

Pretend that you have developed a super-power. What might happen? Would there be difficulties? How did everyone find out? How would you use it? As an eight year-old, I partly believed that I was a prince from another planet. I had been sent here, my memory wiped clean, to be tested out, to be prepared to rule my kingdom. When I was alone I used to talk to those watching me. I developed a series of secret signals and words to open up my communication channel with the 'elders' from my other world. Maybe all of us at one time or another have felt there might be more to us than meets the eye.

Children delight in the idea of exploring a fantasy which gives them power. The writing is more interesting if the power chosen is unusual – such as the ability to throw your voice, make animals talk, or turn people into statues for 20 seconds. *Pippi Longstocking* by Astrid Lindgren is the story of a seven-year-old bionic girl.

Changing places

There are a number of stories in which the main characters change places with someone else – maybe a friend, a parent, or the teacher. The opportunity to step into someone else's shoes offers children new power over their world. Surprisingly, they often fall back on to stereotype views, for example when they choose to be the teacher and start 'whacking' everyone in sight! Careful discussion beforehand about what might work can lead children into exploring deeper concerns and needs. *Freaky Friday* by Mary Rodgers is a useful example.

This idea of swapping places, and the problems – or advantages – that it might bring could begin with a simple exercise: 'If I were an animal I would be a ... because ...' There are many stories about people who have been turned into animals. Look at the fate of Roald Dahl's hero in *The Witches*. He is turned into a mouse.

Becoming a mouse has the attendant problem of size. Children enjoy writing stories in which they have shrunk and see the world from a new perspective. Bottles of coloured water displayed with warning labels, 'A potion to shrink small children', 'A potion to make you grow wings', 'A potion to make you invisible', 'A potion to make you grow tall as a house', and so on, could act as an interesting starting point. You have to choose one of the potions and write a story featuring it. The story might begin with the words 'I raised the drink to my lips and felt a shudder down my spine ...'

The fib

What is the biggest lie that you can think of? What is the biggest lie that you have ever told? What happened? Were you found out? Why did you tell it? How did you feel? This session has to begin with anecdote, or with sheer invention, to tease.

I once told a reception class that I had come to school on an elephant! 'No, you didn't,' they chorused. 'Oh yes', I said, 'It's round the back by the bike sheds and Mr Potts (our school caretaker) is feeding it on packed lunches.' By now some had begun to nod knowingly – yes, they too had seen the elephant.

If you don't want a 'fantasy' session, begin by recalling a time when you told a lie. After hearing pupils' tales, ask them to write a story in which the main focus is the telling of a lie and where it leads. What problems does it create and how are the problems solved?

Another good starting point is to read George Layton's *The Fib* in which the main character tells his friends that his uncle is Bobby Charlton (you can swop the name for a more appropriate well-known footballer if you wish). All goes well until Bobby Charlton comes to town and they come face to face with him ...

Linking objects

There are various ways to present this idea. Basically the writer selects three items and builds a story around them. You might bring in a selection of objects or invite each child to bring in something from home. You could brainstorm some items on to a board. Instead of objects you could have a character, a place, a type of weather and something someone has said. These might be randomly suggested or chosen from a list.

A useful way to begin is by pairs of children planning together how to incorporate the different items into their story. The sorts of objects chosen may well suggest a certain sort of story. For instance, a mirror, a ring and a cloak suggest to me a fairy-tale. Whereas a school bag, a bus ticket and a sleeping bag suggest a story about running away from school. Some of the more intriguing stories occur when the three items selected are quite incongruous – a boiled sweet, an iron and a cricketer's cap, for example.

Quick ideas

Passport

Design and create your own passport with a photo and information about yourself – name, age, date of birth, address, profession, etc. A useful activity for the beginning of term. Or design a passport for a dragon/giant/princess/character from the story you are reading.

Alphabets

Make an alphabet list for the contents of an ogre's pie, a witch's brew, or a dragon's menu, or of excuses for being late, etc.

> A pply – the country's answer to unemployment.
> B ewitched – a hypnotising, forbidden word.
> C andle – ascending light of centuries.
> D ecay – devastation of time . . .
>
> *Richard Tuff, 10 yrs*

Titles

Teachers aren't the only ones who can think of exciting titles for stories. What would your class like to write about? Everyone in the class writes down a list of titles they would like to write about. These can be put on to one sheet of paper and shared out, so everyone can select something new to write about. The best titles are ones that pose a problem, or ask questions, for example, *'My Grandmother's Motorbike.'*

My Grandmother's Motorbike by Cindy Buss

121

An alternative is for everyone to write down a first line for a story. Put these into a hat. Everyone picks out a first line to get them going. The best ones – or at least, the easiest – are openings that grab the reader, that take you straight into the drama. For instance, 'I stretched out my hand into the darkness and felt . . .'

The key

A key can unlock more than a door. A collection of keys is set out, and everyone selects one. What will happen if you use it? What does it open? What is inside? Where does it lead to? Encourage the children to step right into the drama of the story in the first line, for example, 'Sasha turned the key in the lock. The door swung open and with a shriek she fell . . .'.

Horoscope

Look at a series of horoscopes from different newspapers and magazines. Children can then invent their own horoscope for a pet – or for a character in the story they are reading.

Stage five

The Pied Piper of Hamelin

Start by reading Browning's description of the chaos brought about by rats in large numbers:

'Rats!
They fought the dogs and killed the cats,
And bit the babies in the cradles,
And ate the cheeses out of the vats,
And licked the soup from the cooks' own ladles.'

Preliminary discussion and investigation could focus on rats and rat behaviour. Try to discover how rats were first introduced to Europe from the Far East. Consider what advice we might give today to medieval doctors dealing with outbreaks of plague.

Newspaper production

A useful activity is to produce an edition of the *Hamelin Express* considering, first of all, the kind of material that local papers include. You could 'flood' the classroom with old issues and make lists of regular features:

news items
weather forecasts
readers' letters
sports reports
editorials
interviews
'fillers'
cartoons
houses for sale

I prefer to split the class into groups and to appoint an editor for each group, someone I think will be capable of making decisions and keeping cool under pressure. It is the editor's job to distribute tasks and make use of the talents of his staff. I decide on the groups myself, so that I can consider the talents and abilities of each child and ensure, for example, that all the 'artists' are not congregated in one group.

I then set a publication deadline (usually a week or so ahead) and make it quite clear that the deadline is fixed and non-negotiable! Each group's brief is to produce an edition of their newspaper that will give an insight into rat-infested Hamelin.

Local events need reporting in the newspaper, and these will have to be written carefully, making sure they contain all the necessary details. Again, old newspapers can be examined for reports to be read and discussed. Children should understand that reports contain facts, and not the writer's own opinions. It is a good idea to practise reporting by writing about an event in school – the morning assembly, last week's netball match, a visit from a VIP, etc. These reports should all contain facts which are verifiable by other children who took part in the events.

Often there are enthusiastic parents with typewriters who can be persuaded to give up an afternoon during production week to help type out 'copy'. My only stipulation is that editors should have checked the stories and made sure they are legible, prior to sending them for typing. Be warned, there is often a hectic run up to the deadline!

EDITORIAL

The blame is yours

The citizens of Hamelin are now beginning to rise up against the mayor and his counsellors. There have been huge riots, mothers, daughters, fathers and brothers all roaring, demanding to see the mayor. All this has been caused by rats. The town has been overrun with them. Wherever you turn there's a rat scuttling through some withered leaves or concealing itself in a stagnant ditch. At one of the riots an individual shouted 'the only way to put things to rights would be to get rid of the rats'. When I interviewed one of the maids from the mayors office she said that the mayor and his counsellors were having a meeting and much debating was going on. I myself think the mayor and corporation are to blame. Something must be done and soon.

Editor: R Martin

TWO CITIZENS FOUND DEAD

Two people were found dead under the church bells of Hamelin. A witness saw the disaster.

'I was just walking past the church,' he said, 'And I heard a tremendous ringing and a clang. I turned around and a few feet behind me the bells were lying on the ground. I tried to lift them but they were too heavy.'

Investigations are going on and it is thought that the cause was a rat chewing through the rope and thus causing the deaths.

Reporters: D. Earl & T. Bull.

Model-making

The importance of model-making in school is often talked about in terms of the acquisition of manipulative skills and the development of social skills when children work and discuss together. However, from quite an early age, model-making enables children to identify with whatever model truck, house or landscape they are creating. Thus in the classroom, a model, rather than being an end in itself, can be the starting point for imaginative development in many areas.

Any investigation of *The Pied Piper* must inevitably lead to the question, 'What was Hamelin like?'. A three-dimensional representation might go some way towards an answer.

In the 14th century, Hamelin was a milling town that had grown and flourished on the banks of the River Weser. It was also a market town. These two functions need to be highlighted in any model of the town. Most of the buildings would, of course, be private dwellings and children can be encouraged to collect shoeboxes, etc, to make models of these. Some houses can be made with upper floors overlapping the lower ones. They can be fitted with roofs that are either 'thatched' or covered with corrugated card and then painted. Many children enjoy looking in books for medieval features to incorporate into their houses, to give them a degree of authenticity. Small groups can then work on the important buildings of the town – the mills, town hall, churches – while others make market stalls and wares to sell on them. The River Weser could run through the

Hamelin town model by Freda Gardham C.P. School

Photograph by Alan Jones

model with a bridge or bridges spanning it. A painted background could then be added.

Once the model is complete, it is time to 'bring it to life'.

Discuss who lives in each house. Make a census of the town's population. How many children are there? How many able-bodied men? etc. Now let the children focus on the inhabitants of the houses they made. How have they reacted to the coming of the rats? How has the invasion affected their lives? Write diary extracts to show how daily activity is altered or made difficult by the plague of rats.

> In my house lives a married couple called Mr. Hans Jon Brunner, Mrs. Henrietta Brunner and the children, Master Franz Brunner & Miss Corrina Brunner. The parents are both aged 33. The boy is 13 and the girl is 10. Hans delivers to the shops, Henrietta works in a bakery.
>
> *Natasha Smith*

> **Diary extract**
>
> I was just going up to get some more wine from the storeroom and I found rats among most of the bottles. When I went to get some wine from the barrels, something was blocking the tap and stopping the wine from coming out. I had a look in the barrel and I found a drowned rat.
>
> *Daniel Earl*

Suggest that children might want to join with a partner and try to develop an account of an incident involving both families. Perhaps there is a wedding about to take place between the elder daughter from one house and the son from another. What happens? Do the rats ruin all the plans?

Perhaps one family doesn't get on with another family in the town. Write about the incident or incidents that led to the antagonism. Was it something that happened before the rats arrived, or did the rats precipitate hostilities?

Use the model town to write directions from one place to another. How do you get from the church to the town hall? Which streets do you walk along, which buildings do you pass?

With a group of other children, plan a town guide to Hamelin.

What might attract visitors to the town? Put together a guidebook for one of the churches or the town hall, listing and commenting on the important features.

Picture books

Writing for a younger audience

I like to have a collection of picture books freely available in my own classroom whatever the age of my children. I include everything from *Tintin* and *Asterix* to Anthony Browne, John Burningham, Jan Pienkowski and John Prater.

In a mixed ability class, picture books are a reading activity in which everyone can join in at their own level. John Prater's *The Gift*, for example, is wordless but children at any age enjoy placing their own interpretations on the sequence of pictures that make up the narrative.

In *The Gift*, two children open a large box delivered to their house. The chairs that the box contains have limited appeal, but the box itself becomes a plaything, a means of escape into a fantasy world that they both share. Once inside the box the children are flown out of the house, along railway tracks and past surprised passengers at a station. They are then flown out to sea, and then under the sea where they visit a shipwreck and discover a giant whale. Next they discover land and a jungle with all kinds of possibilities until, following a near accident, they both think of tea and home, only to find themselves speeding back to reality. There's a lovely twist at the end of the book.

A book such as *The Gift* should be shared and discussed, while books that balance words and illustrations offer an introduction to the printed literature that children will be meeting for much of the time.

Once children have had time to become familiar with the available picture books, you could suggest that they try to produce their own. Often this suggestion will come from the children themselves. The objections of those who feel that their writing or drawing is weak may be met by suggesting they work in partnership with another child. Both pictures and writing can then evolve from shared ideas.

This is a good opportunity for children to write for a different audience, i.e., younger children in the school. Before they begin to write they should be aware that they will have the chance to try out their stories in this way.

It is a good idea at this stage to visit infant classrooms and talk to the children about the kind of stories they like. Such elementary market research is rewarding if the authors discover, for example, that most children like their stories to be humorous, and that many enjoy stories about animals. Other infants might say that they like to be involved in the stories, perhaps by lifting flaps to see what is hidden beneath, as with the *Spot* books by Eric Hill. Some of your children might like to make a link with one particular infant and feature him or her in the story.

Many of the stories that the children choose to write will be variations on the books they have been reading. Other children will find it difficult to simplify the story they want to tell and to write in direct language. After all, they've been encouraged throughout their school lives to 'flesh out' their prose to 'make it more interesting', and now they're being asked to do the opposite.

Picture books often contain an element of repetition. In *Goodnight, Owl* by Pat Hutchins, Owl is prevented from sleeping during the day because of the variety of noise from other tree creatures. Each page finishes with the line 'And Owl tried to sleep.' This technique could be employed in the children's own books.

Some children will prefer to draft a complete story before they begin to make decisions as to which sections will appear on each page. Others will prefer to work piecemeal, building up their story as they go along. This may be the best approach for children working together, particularly if there is a straight division of tasks between the illustrations and the writing.

After looking at picture books, children should have discovered that there is no need to employ the same format on each page. Check out Anthony Browne's *Gorilla* or *Willy the Champ*. It should not be assumed that each page contains a picture with writing underneath. Browne shows us a variety of visual techniques which the children could adopt or develop. Pictures should be bold and colourful as well as acting as a visual text in their own right.

Once the book is finished and the type and the layout of the cover decided on, encourage the children to look closely at the kind of information featured on a book cover. Usually there is a synopsis of the storyline along with information about the author/illustrator.

The ability to summarise something in a few words or sentences is a skill worth acquiring. In this instance, children are presented with a meaningful task allowing them to practise that skill.

Details about the author should include date and place of birth, interests, and the names of any other books that he has written/illustrated. The name and address of the publisher could also feature on the cover along with the publisher's emblem, the book's ISBN (International Standard Book Number), and its price.

Reading to an audience

Careful preparation is essential to gain the most benefit from contact with younger children. Once the book is complete, there will be a great desire to rush across to the infants and read it at once, without a moment's thought over the best way to present it. Children should be encouraged to practise reading aloud first, and to discover the best places to pause for effect, or to show the pictures. If it is a joint project, the two authors will need to be clear about who is reading each section.

If it is possible for an adult to listen to the stories at this stage, this can only be beneficial. A willing parent, ready to act as guinea-pig, may be able to make all kinds of suggestions as to how the presentation could be improved, before the actual delivery to the young audience.

Young children like to look at pictures and there should be time for them to linger if they wish, rather than having to move on because of the author's impatience or lack of consideration.

All the children were so pleased that from then on they let mervin join in all their games

Extract from *Mervin the Ghost* by Paul Tiltman and James Tree

Ideas for prose writing

Joyous land

This idea may be used independently or in conjunction with work on *The Pied Piper of Hamelin*. Ask children to think what it might have been like inside the Piper's mountain or on an undiscovered island.

For he led us, he said, to a joyous land,
Joining the town and just at hand,
. . .
The sparrows were brighter than peacocks here,
And their dogs outran our fallow deer,
And honey-bees had lost their stings,
And horses were born with eagles' wings.'

The first part of Coleridge's *Kubla Khan* may also serve as inspirational material.

> There is a temple made of a Cyclops's golden eye in the caves of Marcia. The enchanted gardens of Paradise spread a mystified curse over the fishless sea, whose foam is as white as a wizard's beard and where sea monsters fight . . .
>
> *Julie Cannon*

In the land of Delmenco, butterflies grow on trees, and unicorns grow double horns. The lakes look like glass and glitter in the sunlight. The fish are gold with silver fins. You can swim as fast as a swift can fly.

Steven Field

Children can be encouraged to produce 'travel brochures', highlighting the marvels to be found in their joyous lands.

Strange figures

Again, this may be linked with work on *The Pied Piper*. Robert Browning tells us something about the Piper's eccentricities. Can this be developed further?

He was dressed in a strange and marvellous manner, swathed in robes, one half red and the other yellow. This amazing figure, tall and slim, had round his neck a scarf that was yellow and tinged with red and spiralled round his (almost sacred) body until it came to a pipe, carved elaborately and looking most majestic, hanging there as if by magic. His long bony fingers kept slowly caressing it, as if they were softening some old wound.

His thin face was as pale as snow, fresh from the heavens. His eyes shimmered like cool water on a hot summer day. This mysterious man's laugh seemed to dance like the far off call of a lark. His hair hung loosely round his slender neck. This strange man looked like a beggar, yet an immortal.

Rebecca Martin

There are other 'outsider' figures who may make us stop and stare. Gerald Durrell's 'The Rose-Beetle Man' from *My Family and Other Animals* is worth reading as an example. Consider too, the busker in the shopping arcade.

As he sits beside his checked cap, he plays his old violin. People stride past, others stop to stare at his creased face and his young, forever playing hands. In his cap are seven coins. Boys make rude remarks but he is a very friendly man and would not dream of hurting anybody. It is written in his dim eyes and half smile.

Kerry Dale

Time of day

When reading, children often view descriptive passages as something to be got through before the real story begins. Often in their own writing, descriptions are under-developed, and it is important for children to understand how a well-written descriptive passage can set the scene for a story. A bare-bones narrative needs to be 'fleshed out', so that the reader can feel his way into a story and see what lies behind the writer's thinking.

A useful exercise is to ask children to write about a time of day – early morning, noon, twilight, etc – or to describe how a familiar place may change at different times of the day.

Often holiday sensations remain fixed in the memory and can be written about, for example, a twilight drive from the airport to a hotel, the sunrise seen from an aeroplane, night-driving, or a blazing hot day on the beach.

> I woke early that morning to crickets chirping and the mist along the ground. I got up, dressed and went outside. I walked up the dusty worn track leading to the 'we sell everything' type store half way up the mountain. ... I continued up the track, often stopping to look at the distance I had covered. The sun looked new, glaring between caravans and log-huts scattered across the hill ... It was going to be another hot day.
>
> *Lisa Clapham*
>
> **Arriving in Spain at night**
>
> At last we could see the lights of the village in between the hills. For a long time the lights didn't look any nearer. Then we suddenly plunged into the village. We came through and kept on driving in the potholes. Suddenly the road became smooth and after that we were on a bumpy dirt track. Then we stopped. I could hear the sound of the frogs which was blending with the barking of a dog. It was all so different, and there was too much to take in at once.
>
> *Aaron Turpin*

Extended metaphors

James Reeves writes of the sea as 'a hungry dog':

The sea is a hungry dog,
Giant and grey.
He rolls on the beach all day
With his clashing teeth and shaggy jaws.

Other great forces of nature may be given human or animal characteristics in this way. This can be a useful exercise in extended metaphor, i.e., a comparison is made early on in the piece of writing and then carried through to the end.

After the hurricane winds that swept south-east England in October 1987, Fran wrote about the 'werewolf wind'.

A wolf on the prowl, searching for trouble. Howling, it seizes its prey, an old barn roof. Suddenly the scalp of the barn slips into the bough of a tree. Swish! The windwolf whirls through a window, smashing it. His shining eyes wake a sleeping baby. Now there are two to howl.

Fran Martin

On location

Just as artists often work 'in the field', it can be a useful exercise to write on location. The arrival of a fair or circus is a marvellous chance to observe at first hand and to note down sights, sounds and smells that will enable children to build up a description when they return to the classroom.

I have had first rate writing resulting from visits to the following:

- A turkey farm towards Christmas
- The local art gallery
- A disused railway line
- An empty farmhouse
- Disused air-raid shelters
- Backstage at the theatre
- A fishing fleet in port
- A graveyard
- A rubbish tip
- The Imperial War Museum
- A livestock market
- The shoreline at Dungeness.

Fears

A discussion of fears could take place to start with, where a distinction is made between real and imaginary fears. Real fears might include worrying about a pet being run over, Mum and Dad arguing too often, coming home to an empty house, having injections, spending time in hospital, etc.

Imaginary fears might involve worrying whether someone is hiding under the bed, hearing footsteps on the stairs, Dracula and Frankenstein, or other figures from horror films, etc.

Sometimes it can be revealing and, indeed, therapeutic to encourage children to write about their fears. I try to stress that what is written should be as honest an account as possible, and that no one will laugh because someone has expressed fears which others consider trivial.

> **The first thing I can remember that frightened me**
>
> The first thing I can remember that frightened me was the rain and thunder and lightning. The rain used to frighten me because it used to make noises on my window pane. When I used to hear thunder I would go under my covers at night and sweat. I always cried and my mum used to take me into her bed. I liked that because my mum could protect me and I knew I was safe.
>
> *Karen Evans, 9 yrs.*

It is really quite difficult for children to write scary stories that are effective. The problem for much of the time is one of overstatement, with nothing being left to the reader's imagination. Encourage children to think and talk about any of the early black-and-white 'horror' films they've seen. Discuss the effectiveness of the various techniques that were employed to build up an atmosphere of suspense – a door-handle slowly turning, heavy footsteps coming closer, something being dragged over the floor, etc. How can children evoke a similar atmosphere in their own descriptions?

When the children are writing their own accounts, continue to emphasise that you are not looking for a horror story, and that subtlety is important when building a mood. Rebecca handles her encounter with a strange manifestation in a capable manner:

... He looked like a priest or some strange religious preacher. He moved towards the chest, opened it and looked at the paper. Then he spoke with a voice that seemed crumpled with age. He said, 'You have disturbed the ladder of time. This is the key to freedom, the answer to all questions.' Then he disappeared. Fran and I didn't understand, but a strange eeriness seemed to make the air suffocating. The finger of death seemed to reach out and touch our very breath. Then we felt ourselves falling, falling through time and space. Suddenly we stopped and we were lying on the grass borders of Scotney Castle.

*From **The Finger of Death** by Rebecca Martin, 11 yrs.*

Late for school

Suggest that children write a 'tall story', in this instance a fantastic and convoluted reason for being late for school.

It is a good idea to consider first tall stories in general, and if possible read some of the tales of Baron Munchausen.

You could also read the poem *Late for School* by Judith Nicholls in her collection *Magic Mirror* (Faber) or in the anthology *Marbles in my Pocket* (Macmillan).

Perhaps children would prefer to explore why someone else was late for school.

This morning I was late for school because there was a knock on my door and I opened it to find that the local farmer had just dumped a lorry load of horse manure on our doorstep. I had to dig myself a route to the front gate.

This morning my teacher was late for school because his wife was tired of exercise books on her coffee table and catapulted them all into the kitchen waste-bin. He had to remove all the potato peelings that had become lodged between the pages like bookmarks.

This morning my headmaster was late for school because his Lotus Elan was jammed at the lights when the star performers from Sid Serrendipity's Travelling Flea Circus had escaped. They had to be hunted down and recaptured before the traffic could move.

Atlantis

The notion of a once-powerful empire that sank beneath the sea has immense appeal for children. Did it ever exist? What is known about it? Could it have happened? Children enjoy inventing reasons why Atlantis sank beneath the waves. In the example below, Nadia uses the Old Testament 'wrath of God' to explain why the catastrophe occurred.

> There was once a race of people who were so conceited they were unbearable to talk to. If they weren't boasting about how strong they were, they were boasting about how clever they were. They were called Doshas. They had a leader who was more conceited than all his people put together, his name was Mishacan.
>
> Mishacan lived in a palace which overlooked the city that his people inhabited. One day God decided that he had had enough of Mishacan so he told him that if he didn't mend his ways within nine days, his city would sink to the ocean floor. Mishacan just laughed at God and God became angrier still and said that he would make it sink now.
>
> God raised his hand and the city began to sink. Mishacan ran to his palace window where he was just in time to see his city sink. Mishacan was sorry for what he had done, he pleaded with God to let his city rise again but God said that if he wanted to see his city he would have to sacrifice his body to being a bubble round the city so that his people could breathe. 'You will always be able to see your people but never talk to them'.
>
> And that is how Atlantis came about.
>
> *Nadia Bagwell, 10 yrs*

Other 'legends' could be written, in an attempt to explain such mysteries as UFOs, Stonehenge, the Yeti, the creature in Loch Ness, etc. Also look at different legends from around the world.

Reviewing

A good starting point is to look at examples of book, film and TV reviews in the local and national press. See if children can work out any themes common to most reviews. With books there's usually something about the story or content, and then often an attempt to set the new work within the context of the author's earlier body of work. This kind of pattern could be followed in the classroom where children have been regularly exposed to literature. Is the author's new book up to the standard of his/ her other books? Finally, how is the book rated? Is it a good read, would you recommend it? Does it reach out and grab you from the opening paragraph, or do you need to stay with it for a while before you are hooked?

Book Review: The Thought Domain by Paul Stewart

Neil (the hero of this story) suddenly gets whisked away to a strange new world where nothing is as it seems. It is the Thought Domain. The future of the world lies in Neil's hands and his quest to defy the evil Gander leads him into some hilarious and some frightening situations.

The story is very well thought out and the adventures that Neil and his friends Ship Shape and Shambles undertake are completely different. I think that this gives it certain qualities that other books just don't have.

I think that the whole idea of a Thought Domain where all the thoughts of everyone who ever lived are stored, is a very original one.

The book has a striking cover and is beautifully illustrated. My only complaint is that the book has a bit of an abrupt ending. Overall it has a distinct air of magic and laughter. I think it is a superb book, wonderful.

Rebecca Martin, 11 yrs

Film/Video Review: Ghostbusters

'Ghostbusters' is a film about three men who were thrown out of a Manhattan college. They soon find that they are broke. They hit on the idea of starting a business called 'Ghostbusters' – an organization that kills off ghosts for money. They start by putting three mortgages on one of their gang's houses and then comfort him by persuading him that everyone has three mortgages nowadays.

In the next three months, Ghostbusters becomes famous, they feature in every paper and on every channel of radio and television. Everyone is going ghost crazy. Ghostbusters are being hired all over the U.S.A. Wherever they go they are mobbed by the media.

At one point they are investigating a ghost in a library. 'Listen,' says Spengler, the brains behind Ghostbusters. Stantz and Venkman whirl round to face him, nerves stretched almost to snapping point. They say in unison, 'What?' 'Can you smell something?'

They find a sticky liquid dripping off a filing cabinet drawer. 'Take a sample,' says Spengler. 'God,' says Stantz, 'Someone blows their nose and you want to take a sample!'

This film has been a hit in America and is well on the way to being a hit here too. I think it's rather far-fetched but very funny and it has good special effects. It's well worth a visit.

Neal Heffernan, 11 yrs

Remember that a reviewer needs to know just how much of the storyline of a book or film he should give away. The ending should certainly not be revealed, although sometimes there are pointers as to what happens, i.e., 'Have a box of tissues handy', or 'Not for the squeamish'.

Headlines

Children often enjoy writing alternative stories for some of the more bizarre headlines that appear in the tabloids or local papers. If nothing suitable is found, engaging headlines can be composed and stories written to support them.

Bank Job Committed by Daughter of Sussex Vicar

A daughter of a vicar has been tried and found guilty by Lewes Crown Court. Along with three men she was accused of armed robbery and other smaller crimes in and around the area. She and one of the men were found hiding loot in the crypt of her father's church. The vicar is believed to be in shock and is 'praying to God for her forgiveness'.

After the verdict the judge said to reporters, 'This is an appalling crime, using the resting place of the dead as a store house for stolen goods. She deserved what she got.'

The stolen money has now been returned to the bank.

Theresa Balcombe 12 yrs

Quick ideas

How my brother/sister gets out of the washing up

A chance to complain and to expose feeble excuses for what

they really are. If you're an only child, then confess how you escape the household chores. Try to limit this to a paragraph, and make it humorous.

A police car called at the school today and took away the caretaker/cook/headmaster

Choose either to relate the events that led up to this, or to tell what follows on. How do other people react to the news? What kind of crime has been committed, or is it all a case of mistaken identity?

Message in a bottle

While walking along the seashore you discover a bottle complete with message. What does it say? Who sent it? Is there a story to be written about the bottle, or is the message a story in itself? Remember that in the time of Queen Elizabeth I, it was an offence punishable by death to open a bottle that contained a message.

Other people's gardens

What is the fascination in staring into other people's gardens? Are we comparing them with our own gardens, or with an ideal garden that exists in the pages of literature?

Try to write a comparison between your garden and one that you see regularly, which is strikingly different to yours. Bring in humour if you wish.

Presenting an argument

A sum of money has been made available to your town or village for the purpose of buying equipment for either a) young mothers, b) teenagers, c) senior citizens. Try to think how each party would put their case when bidding for the money.

Stage six

Historical fiction

An exploration of similar themes in fiction for children – World War II

- *Fireweed* and *The Dolphin Crossing* by Jill Paton Walsh.
- *The Machine Gunners* by Robert Westall.
- *Friend or Foe* by Michael Morpurgo.
- *Carrie's War* by Nina Bawden.
- *Goodnight Mister Tom* by Michelle Magorian.
- *I am David* by Anne Holm.
- *The Silver Sword* by Ian Serraillier.
- *Rose Blanche* by Christopher Gallaz and Ian McEwan, illustrated by Roberto Innocenti.
- *How's Business* by Alison Prince.

An alternative to the shared exploration of a single work of fiction is to consider a group of books on similar themes. I find this approach works particularly well with historical fiction, and will initiate or complement further research into a certain period of time. It is impossible to start to read *Fireweed* or *Carries' War*, for example, without some preliminary exploration of the Home Front.

Questioning grandparents and listening to wartime anecdotes will prove far more valuable than the simple listing of dates and facts. How far back is fifty years? Older children should be gaining some appreciation of the concept of time, but grandparents and elderly relatives can provide an actual link with the past, i.e., fifty years ago was when Grandad was a lad.

Similarly, making a collection of artefacts – medals, information leaflets, photographs, shell cases, perhaps a gas mask, can lead on to further worthwhile investigation.

Wartime advertisements may be examined and their effectiveness considered. Children may be eager to write their own slogans: 'Definitely no second helpings – there's a war on.' Others may be re-interpreted pictorially. Much discussion can take place as to how the landscape was transformed in wartime. Think about the sights of war that would have been familiar to

141

children – barrage balloons, taped windows, queues for food, bombsites, etc. A school caretaker who had lived in the town all his life came to talk about the changes he remembered when, as a lad of thirteen, the war began and his lifestyle was drastically altered.

One particular anecdote involved his mother, who had been peeling potatoes by the kitchen window when a German fighter pilot parachuted down into a field close by. With the knife in her hand, she raced along to the field where the parachutist informed her that Hitler would be dining in Buckingham Palace in six months' time!

The children who heard the story were quick to reproduce the incident in cartoon form, using balloon captions for the pilot's words and the mother's reply.

Cartoon by Fran Martin

This 'storyboard' technique can be used to order and highlight the important moments in any fictional account, for example the moment in *Fireweed* when an unexploded bomb is discovered in Bill's aunt's back garden, or the initial meeting between Rudi and the children in *The Machine Gunners*.

Fireweed is the story of Bill and Julie, two runaways who meet at the height of the London Blitz. At first, trying to get by and escape detection in the ruined city is fun, but gradually they are troubled by guilt and burdened with responsibilities.

Bill and Julie have both run away from unsuccessful attempts to evacuate them – Bill from an unhappy life in Wales and Julie after the failure to 'seavacuate' children to Canada.

Other accounts of evacuation can be found in *Friend or Foe* and *Carrie's War*, but it is perhaps best to explain the whole concept by relating it to the children themselves:

'Imagine coming to school with your suitcase, sandwiches and gas mask, and walking to the station wearing a label with your name and address on. Imagine boarding a train with many other children and travelling for hours and hours, stopping and starting again and again, until you finally reach your destination where you're taken to some village hall and handed over to strangers, or worse still, made to stand in a bunch while the strangers pick you out one by one.'

You can attempt to establish an empathy with these children who left their homes and families, by discussing the notion of separation and all that it entails. Those who have had experience of being away from home, even for short periods, will be able to relate their feelings. Can the children imagine being evacuees, unsure if they will ever see their homes or parents again?

I try to encourage writing at this stage. What would it be like staying with a different family and attending another school? Who would you miss if you had to leave home? What would you miss? What would you take with you to remind you of home?

We had to leave home because it was being knocked down. Everything was packed and we were ready to go. I looked back and thought of all the things I'd miss. The den in the cellar that was once full of coal until we got rid of it when we had central heating put in, but it was always full of coal dust. The window stickers that had lost their stick, but I kept them to remind me of the summer my brother was born and I went to the R. S. P. C. A. courses. The sooty fireplaces that were never used except for the one in the front room that was only used at Christmas. The creaky stairs that Louis and I mended when I was three. The cracks between the floorboards in the front room, the bathroom that I stripped so many years ago. My large bedroom that was full of posters and Lego. My brother's bedroom that was mine for over six years, the room with memories of when I was small. The bedroom that is no one's and never has been since we were here. The tree in the garden that held my rope and swing. But now this and much more is over and gone.

Aaron Turpin, 10 yrs.

It is better still if we can bring alive the notion of evacuation, by inviting evacuees into the classroom to talk about their experiences. Children's grandparents or school staff members may have their own stories to relate. A meeting with someone who was 'really there' is of immense value in forging links with the past. (On one occasion, my then head teacher spoke about his evacuation from Guernsey to Bradford, three weeks before the German invasion of the Channel Islands.) A useful collection of memories is *No Time to Wave Goodbye* by Ben Wicks.

Neither the evacuees or their parents knew where they were being taken. One of the children's first tasks on arrival was to write a postcard home, giving a brief message and the postal address. Children can be asked to imagine what might have been written on Carrie's first postcard home:

Dear Mummy and Daddy,

I miss you very much. The journey here was awful, about half our school, all squeezed into one tiny carriage. When we eventually reached Wales we went to the village hall (it was a good job you packed that extra drink, I might have died without it). Don't tell anyone about this but I was terrified Nick and I were going to be split up but we were lucky. The people we are staying with are called Miss Evans and Mr Evans. Nick cried most of the first night but he is settling in OK now. Here it doesn't seem as though there's a war on except for the black-outs and the rationing of course. We have been quite well accepted in our new school, there's been a few fights but they soon blow over. I really do miss you and I can't wait till this stupid war is over and we can come home again.

All my love, Carrie

P.S. Nick sends his love and our new address is: c/o Samuel Isaac Evans, High St, Pontypridd, Wales.

Rebecca Martin, 11 yrs

Children could be asked to list the reasons that might make them take the desperate step of running away from their new home. Read the first few pages of *The Dolphin Crossing*, where an evacuee is being taunted by village lads. Consider where you would run to, and how you'd travel. Read Bill's account of his escape in *Fireweed*. Some children might like to write a day-by-day diary of an escape attempt. What would be your parents' reaction if you turned up unexpectedly in the middle of an air raid?

You could follow this by reading the first few pages of *Goodnight Mister Tom* which show us that evacuation was welcomed by some children, who escaped from dreadful conditions in their own homes. Consider what kind of life Willie left behind him.

Through Willie Beech in *Goodnight Mister Tom*, we learn that people die in war and that the way to accept a death is not through grieving, but through allowing the good qualities in someone to live on in you. Willie takes a long time to come to this realisation, but it is much easier for him to cope with his friend's death once he does.

In both *The Machine Gunners* and *Friend or Foe*, children find themselves in situations where it is necessary to re-evaluate the received viewpoint. All through our lives we are constantly having to re-evaluate our view of others in the light of their conduct or behaviour. By asking children to examine fictional dilemmas from every angle, we are helping them develop a valuable skill.

In *The Machine Gunners*, Chas McGill finds a crashed Heinkel, a dead German and a machine-gun plus ammunition. The gun is then hidden from the authorities, who suspect that it has fallen into the wrong hands but are unable to prove anything. Eventually the gun becomes the centrepiece of an elaborate camp that Chas and his friends construct.

Rudi is a rear gunner who parachutes from his plane when it is hit on a bombing raid. He sprains his ankle on landing, and after a week or two of foraging in allotments and garden sheds, he stumbles across a doorway in a mound of rubble which turns out to be the entrance to Chas's camp. He steps inside and finds himself looking into the barrel of a machine-gun.

This is an excellent place at which to pause for the question, 'What do you think happens next?'.

In *Friend or Foe* two evacuees, David and Tucky, are convinced that a German plane crash-landed near their new home, but despite an extensive search of the surrounding hills by the authorities, nothing is discovered. The two boys search the hills themselves but disaster strikes when David falls into a stream and is near to drowning. He is rescued by one of the two Germans from the crashed aircraft. When David has recovered the Germans plead for help, for food and blankets. One of them is injured and cannot travel, but with time they hope to make their escape. What should the boys do? 'He saved your life Davey,' says Tucky, 'we've got to help.'

An 'understanding' develops between the two boys and the two Germans. Each learns something from the other. Similarly, in *The Machine Gunners*, Rudi and the children form a 'friendship' that transcends frontiers, language barriers, and 'sides'.

Aside from the moral dilemmas posed by the concept of war itself, there are marvellous opportunities here to explore the 'grey areas' between right and wrong.

Most children will opt firmly for one side or the other. Reasons can be written down. It is even more valuable if children can stand back from their own preferences and list the reasons why both courses of action might be adopted, i.e., helping the enemy or turning him over to the authorities. The ability to examine a problem from both sides is worth acquiring.

It might be interesting at this point to read a brief extract from *Albeson and the Germans* by Jan Needle, where Albeson's views of the Germans who are about to visit his school are influenced by the war comics he is always reading. War comics, after all, offer us stereotypes, and it can be hard at times to see beyond them.

Rose Blanche is a picture book by Roberto Innocenti, with a text by Christopher Gallaz and Ian McEwan. This is a book to use alongside *The Silver Sword* and *I am David*, although the latter book is timeless and not directly linked with World War II.

Rose Blanche is a young German girl who discovers the location of a concentration camp for children on the outskirts of her town. She brings them food until one day, as the war draws to an end, the camp and the children vanish. This book will probably spark off a huge amount of discussion concerning the effects of the war in Europe and the treatment of minorities and those who opposed the Nazi regime. It serves as an antidote to the 'happy endings' of *The Silver Sword* and *I am David*, reminding us that the Second World War, for millions of families, was a time of great unhappiness.

Autobiography

If I were to write my earliest memories, there would be two incidents dating back to my third year. One is moving house. We only moved across the road so no removal van was needed, just countless trips from our old house to the new one. I can remember crossing the road swinging a saucepan in each hand, doing my bit to help.

My second memory is of the street party that was organised for Coronation Day, June 1953, although I'm not sure whether I really do remember this event or whether I only think I do because of photos in the family album.

How far back can children remember? Some will need prompting to remember anything further back than their last birthday, while others will recall a whole host of memories. Some children will probably claim to remember events that happened when they were in their prams. This could lead to discussion as to how much is real recall, and how much is based on family photographs.

A time line can be useful, particularly if it is put together with the help of parents, filling in dates and details such as when

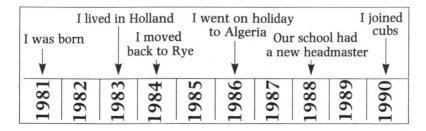

brothers or sisters were born, when the family moved house, when and where the family spent their holidays, etc.

An amusing lead into a piece of writing on earliest memories is for the class to bring to school photographs of themselves as babies or toddlers. These can be fixed to the wall and made into a quiz (add one of yourself, too!).

The writing of autobiographical incidents can have particular relevance when children are about to leave one school and enter another, or as a first activity at the new school.

To make it easier I usually divide the writing into three sections – pre-school, infant or first school, and junior or middle school. Prior to writing, children will appreciate hearing your memories and perhaps those from an author who has published his own autobiography. I've taken extracts from *Cider with Rosie* by Laurie Lee (the early chapters), and from *Boy* by Roald Dahl (although Dahl claims that this isn't an autobiography). The latter's recollections in 'The Bicycle and the Sweet Shop' (chapter 3) are particularly well received.

Children should be encouraged to think of two or three incidents that they remember well. In the pre-school section the incidents might be a friendship at playgroup, an outing, a special toy, a pet, the first time they tasted candyfloss/hot dogs/ peppermint icecream, the first thing that frightened them, or an accident of some kind.

Hated that day in Dad's office
when the slammer came down on my fingers.
Blood spilling everywhere, went in the
office car.
At hospital I had eight stitches.

Paul Tiltman, 10 yrs

An odd thing that I do remember because I was very young then. I remember eating chocolate mousse in my playpen while the grown ups were sitting round the table for lunch.

Maria Stanford, 13 yrs

Reminiscing about infant and junior school should precede writing, particularly if children were pupils at different schools.

Some will need prompting. What do you remember about your teachers? What books did you read? Can you remember any school trips? Who were your friends? Was there anyone you didn't get on with very well? Were you away from school with any childhood illnesses? Did you go anywhere special on holiday? Were you ever in danger?

In the piece below, Claire really makes us live through her moment of danger.

Once I experienced just about the most frightening thing that could happen to a girl of ten.

My sister Gillian and I go to a friend of my mums for six and a half hours when mum is at work. Her name is Debbie. She has three children. Leon, a four year old boy, Nathan a seven year old boy, and Alexina (Alex) a ten year old girl.

We all wanted to go to the Wish Tower to see the Radio 1 Roadshow. Unfortunately, when we got there it had finished, so we stayed on the beach. We ate some of our delicious picnic, got changed for swimming and ran off into the sea. Leon and Gillian paddled in the shallow waters while us bigger children waded up to our waists. We discovered that the wind was blowing up some pretty big waves. Every time that a wave came near us all we jumped it. Soon two big waves came leaping at us together. They pushed me back further towards the shore of the next beach! I started to wade back when suddenly the sand disappeared beneath my feet. I had got myself into a hole. I tried to swim back to the shallow waters but the current and the wind overpowered me and pushed me onto a stony, barnacle covered groyne separating our beach from the next.
'Help, help, I can't swim, I'm stuck, help me, please,' I cried. I can swim quite well but I was useless against the strong waves.
'Claire, are you O.K.' shouted Nathan.
'No, I'm stuck,' I shouted. (He waded over and then a huge wave swept him into the hole. He gulped and gasped as his head went underwater. He grabbed hold of my waist.
'Nathan, Nathan, you're pulling me under,' I cried.
'I can't swim,' he shouted back.

We both reached for the groyne and hoisted ourselves up onto it. Now we were definitely in a mess. Everytime a wave came, it bashed us unmercifully against the groyne. We were both screaming and crying now.

Alex heard us. She came over and got stuck. She ended up on the groyne too. We all screamed and cried for help. Two girls of about 14 or 15 were laughing and playing a little way away. They thought we were just laughing and so did Debbie.

Suddenly we did start laughing and we all became hysterical with sheer fright. Then we saw our cut and bleeding legs and arms from the barnacles on the groyne. This set us off crying again. This made the two girls realise that we needed help and fast. They both rushed over to us with such looks on their faces that it reminded me of all the films you watch where kids drown. At the end you see a slow-motion replay of the parents running with agony written all over their faces. I saw Leon and Gillian race over to Debbie while the two girls came nearer. Debbie suddenly kicked off her sandals and raced like wildfire into the sea, fully clothed! She had the agony look on her face which made me go into hysterics again. She put an arm round Nathan and me. She lugged us into the shallow waters but even then I was not going to let go of her. The two girls carried Alex back. Debbie wrapped us up and noticed that I had the most cuts. I had been there longest. Alex and Nathan and a few on their stomachs but I had cuts all over my legs and arms. Blood was everywhere ...

Claire Banner, 11 yrs

Another angle of approach is for the children to consider how they see themselves, and then how they think others see them. 'A school report on myself' can prompt some honest writing, as strengths and weaknesses are evaluated.

Then get them to consider the views of others: Mum, Dad, grandparents, brothers, sisters, best friend, etc. How do they see you? 'My mum thinks I'm ...'

Finally, what makes you unique? How are you different from your friends? List some of the ways in which you think that you are different from others.

Ideas for prose writing

Running away

This has been successfully explored in a number of children's novels and recently in the award winning *The Runaways* by Ruth Thomas. In this story two 'ugly duckling' children, a white girl and a black boy, are caught up in the same trouble where the only way out is to run away. Gradually the early animosity between the two children is replaced by a grudging respect for each other's abilities, and eventually by friendship, as they endure and survive the hazards of being on the run.

The notion of running away to avoid facing up to problems is one that children will be drawn to. Various questions can be asked. Can you think of a situation where you might think running away is the only solution? Where would you go if you did run away? How would you survive? (Ruth Thomas's runaways had plenty of money!) Who would suffer from the results of such a drastic course of action?

Some good local detail might be worked into a story about spending a day away from school. Where are the local hiding places? One problem with writing this kind of story, and indeed any other, is to ensure a realistic passage of time. For example –

I took a look at my watch as I arrived at my camp. It was 9.30 a.m.

Then one incident later – a conversation with a neighbour who obviously suspects something – the story continues:

By this time it was 2.30 p.m. and I decided to take a chance and go into the town.

Time passing has to be explained away satisfactorily. Where does it go? Doesn't it seem to go much more slowly when you're on your own anyway?

If you decide to run away with a friend, this is a good chance to develop the relationship between you. Are you both as keen to 'bunk off', or is one of you very persuasive? Who gets cold feet first? Does your friendship survive the incident or are you changed by it in some way? What about the outcome – at school, your parents' reactions, etc. Perhaps in the end you're not quite so sure why you ran away in the first place!

My head was in a whirl, I wanted to find my Mum. But that's why I had run away, to get away from my Mum!

Letter-writing

To many children, letter-writing is a chore only to be undertaken with great reluctance when relations need thanking for Christmas and birthday gifts. The first sentence is easy, 'Thank you very much for ...', but after a while comes the familiar cry of 'I don't know what to write'.

It is important to practise letter-writing, as it involves an awareness of different styles of writing. Children need to choose an appropriate 'voice', depending on who they are writing to. They wouldn't expect to write to an elderly aunt in the same way as to a friend.

Formal letters in the classroom should be purposeful. They should be real letters which are being written to seek information, perhaps for a project. They should be courteous, carefully thought out and neatly written. You are asking a favour of the reader, so thank him/her in anticipation.

Much information for a local study can be gained by writing to local firms about their products, their markets, why they choose to site themselves in the area, etc. Most will take the time to write back, and some will be very helpful indeed.

It is also worth acquiring a copy of *Free Stuff for Kids* (Exley Publications). This provides a valuable list of possible recipients for letters.

Authors enjoy receiving letters from members of their reading public. Again, most will take time to reply, particularly if there are questions to be answered. However, ensure that all the children are not writing to the same author! If the author's home address isn't known, letters may be sent to the author's publisher who will forward them.

There are other occasions for meaningful letter-writing activities. There may have been important visitors in the school. Children will see the necessity of thanking people who have given up their time to come into school. Invitations can be written to parents asking them to visit the school on open days, or to other classes asking them to come and watch some drama or listen to some music.

Children should realise that newspapers, radio and TV can

Woodingdean Primary School
Warren Road,
Woodingdean

13th October

Dear Mr Moses,

Thank you for coming and reading all those poems to us. I thought poetry was boring I didn't know there was a funny side to poetry. I liked the race and the Vampire poem. Our class have been writing lots of poems since I liked the way you read the poems as if they were really happening. I hope you came again.

Yours Sincerely
michele Carney

Letter by Michele Carney

provide a platform from which important local and national issues may be debated. How would they feel if test drillings for oil were about to take place in their local area, or if the government was considering dumping nuclear waste nearby or building a motorway close to their school?

Finally, consider other examples of letter-writing – letters from the Front (soldiers' letters from World War I and II), 'The Tolkien Letters', Spike Milligan's published letters, etc.

Monsters

It is difficult to write convincingly about monsters. Sometimes our attempts with words are as clumsy as those efforts of early film-makers, trying to film dinosaurs fighting in a lost world.

In her book *The Brothers Lionheart*, Astrid Lindgren describes a fight between Katla, a terrible she-dragon and Karm, a dreadful sea serpent:

'But then we saw the serpent. He raised his green head out of the foam and his tail whipped up the water; oh he was terrible, a giant serpent, as long as the river is wide . . . and then he saw Katla. She floated up out of the depths and was suddenly in the middle of the whirlpools, and the serpent threw himself headlong at her and coiled himself around her'.

Often the descriptions of monsters by children are little more than catalogue listings of how many eyes, legs or heads the creatures have. Some subscribe to the theory that a creature with five hundred heads must be five hundred times as awful as one with a single head!

Far more important when creating a monster in words is to describe its total appearance, using all the senses. What does it look like? Can you compare it with anything? What would its skin feel like if you touched it? What sort of noise does it make? How does it move along? Has it got a dreadful smell? How does it revolt you?

In the piece below, Claire succeeds in presenting a graphic description of the ancient Egyptian horror called 'The Devourer'.

The Devourer

The Devourer has a crinkled, slimy body. Its might is amazing, it could tear a stone like tissue paper, it's worse than any nightmare when it's peering down at you. It has a long lashing tongue like a whip but sharper and purple as it comes out of its mouth. It's worse than a sword coming down on you, it has a screamy, screechy noise and the odd snort, so loud that it deafens you.

It's so ugly that most girls, or boys for that matter, would die at the sight of it. All over it is totally thick, oozing slime coming out of holes in its body. Its nose has spikes which are very poisonous. Its breath is deadly and a horrible purply-green colour. If you touch it and IT is the only thing to say, you will get caught in its slime and be sucked into its body through the nasty slime because it doesn't eat through its mouth.

If you see in its one single nostril there's blood dripping off cobwebs and beyond that is fire, fire roaring inside it. The fire screams at you and you feel you're in there and you're running. Wherever you look there's fire, round and round, you get dizzy, then you wake up and you've been hypnotised. Then you see it staring at you with its nightmare eyes, big, flabby and disgusting. It breathes steam which stinks awfully. Its teeth are daggers with blood on them and blood flows from its mouth like a stream. If you get caught and go inside this devil's body, it's said to be worse than being thrown into a pit with poisonous snakes. If you ever see this awful creature, beware, because your mind and eyes will never see anything or hear or smell or think of anything but IT.

Claire Bayntun, 10 yrs

Complaints

Are there aspects of your lifestyle or your parents' lifestyle that annoy you? This is often a cause of family friction as well as being an important issue in much fiction for children. Perhaps Dad or Mum spend too much time tinkering with the car or worrying about prize blooms in the garden, or following a hobby that affects the lives of everyone else in the house. For example, perhaps each weekend you're bundled into the car and driven for miles so that you can watch other cars being driven round a circuit!

In the following piece, Josie complains about her mum's passion for healthy eating:

I've got friends who get home from school and have fish fingers and chips and beans and things like that. Not me. I say, what've we got tonight mummy? Stir-fried vegetables and chicken or fillet of lamb in lemon with herbs, lentil pancakes with coleslaw, meatballs with pitta bread and salad. When we go out for a treat, it's not for a Wimpy, it's lamb pasanda or seafood pasta. My sister used to say, 'Yuk! I hate mushrooms, red peppers, curry,' but now she knows if she doesn't eat it she won't get anything. As well as all that there's salad – lamb's lettuce, radicchio, watercress, chicory, endive, fennel – with dressing. I've got friends who have Angel Delight, or semolina for pudding. I have Greek yogurt with honey and things I can't even spell! But then if Mummy has yoga or we have badminton coaching and we're in a rush, we might still have fish fingers and beans!

Josie Farrow, 11 yrs

People

Children need help with developing characters. Lots of character sketch exercises can be tried out. Younger children find pictures useful to relate to. You can use photographs, or pictures cut from magazines, catalogues, etc, and build up an identity for each. This can work well in a group situation. Remember that people are multi-dimensional, and that this should be borne in mind when characters are being developed.

As children develop their characters they should try to add small details that bring them to life. Think about physical characteristics, personal preferences, hobbies, quirks, where they live and why, etc. Then try to explain how these features affect the characters' lifestyles.

Writing about friends or family members is a good exercise in character development. The two accounts below are both of grandparents, and both writers manage to produce some small but significant details that really bring their subjects to life. Natasha writes about her grandad's fluffy white moustache and the way his eyes used to fill with water. Adrian tells how he and his granny both wear the same size shoes.

My Grandad was one of the kindest people I ever knew. His fluffy white moustache used to tickle when he kissed me. His laugh was like Father Christmas's chuckle. He taught my brother and me how to play darts. My Grandad and Grandma made the best sausage rolls in the world. To me there was a special way how he used to express his happiness, his eyes used to fill up with water, but not tears, just happiness. He was chubby and had snow white hair. His glasses for reading balanced perfectly on his nose. My daddy took after him in one thing, his height, he was small. But all that is left of him now is just memories.

Natasha Smith, 11 yrs

My granny lives near Wakefield in Yorkshire in a semi-detached house with my grandad and my auntie Sue. My granny is not very tall. She is about five foot high. She has dark curly hair which she always cuts herself and never goes to the hairdressers. My granny is a diabetic so she has a special diet. Although I am only nine and a half years old we can both wear my size four shoes.

Adrian Harris, 9 yrs

156

One-sided telephone conversations

My house backs on to a road where there is a telephone box which is frequently used by holidaymakers from the local caravan sites. As in many of the older phone boxes, much of the glass is missing.

It seems that many of the people who make use of the phone box are doubtful of British Telecom's ability to transmit calls properly, so they shout into the mouthpiece and so relay their message to the neighbourhood.

I've eavesdropped on a number of delightful one-sided telephone conversations, and it can be an interesting exercise to try to write one yourself. This is an idea that needs careful thought. Children need to be reminded that they are only writing one side of a conversation but that it should be phrased in such a way that the reader can follow what is being said at the other end of the line.

Discuss situations where they might find themselves listening to a one-sided conversation – in a hospital lobby where a proud father is ringing his family, or on a railway station where a commuter is explaining to his wife that he'll be late home yet again.

Hello.
It's me!
I'm, sort of, well, at the police station.
Well, I sort of..., well, you know what it's like.
I was, sort of, driving.
I know I'm only twelve.
It was an accident, I knocked against the key.
Well, it was Andrew.
Andrew's a mate of mine.
He's perfectly alright.
Wasn't his fault.
It wasn't mine.
It was the keys ... it sort of, moved.
I'm alright.
Well, it's in the pond.
I'm not a very good steerer and I couldn't see through the chickens that were in the market.
They're in the pond as well.
This really nice policeman said that you could pay for the damages.

Language!
Oh thanks! See you in a minute then.
Bye.
Yes . . . bye, okay!
Bye then . . .
See you soon.

Theresa Balcombe, 13 yrs.

A good start

Many factors influence us when we pick up a book and decide whether we wish to read it or not. Many people read the first paragraph or the first page and make a decision on the basis of how well it grips their attention. Making a good start in a story is important, and a worthwhile exercise is to write what might be the starting paragraph of a story.

A story might begin with a quirky piece of dialogue or with the kind of statement that makes you want to say to the author, *'Oh yes, well prove it!'*. For example, *'The Herdmans were absolutely the worst kids in the history of the world.'* (from *The Worst Kids in the World* by Barbara Robinson).

Bernard Ashley begins *Break in the Sun* with the kind of statement that reaches out and grabs you, *'Two people had secrets up on the roof of Riverside School'*.

Below are the starting paragraphs of two lengthy stories written by eleven-year-old girls. The first account begins well with a leading question, but then trails off into a rather lame description.

The second account brings us into the action straight away. A noise in the night has woken Tom. We discover that he's a boy with an imagination, who can't resist the chance to investigate something suspicious.

The Time Room

Chapter one: The House on the Hill

'Why don't we go and explore the house on the hill Pat?' said Amy. She was about five foot three inches, had brunette hair and blue eyes, unlike her sister who was about five foot nine and had black hair and brown eyes.
'O.K. Amy, we might as well because we've got nothing to do.'

'When shall we leave?' said Amy, for she was very eager.
'In about ten minutes. I'll get mum to make us some
sandwiches and buy us some coke and then we can have a
picnic lunch.'
'Great,' said Amy, while she wondered what they were going
to find.

Tom's Secret Dragon

Chapter one: The Arrival

'What was that?' said Tom, sitting up in bed quickly. He had
heard a kind of SPLAT, BONG, as if something heavy, actually
extremely heavy, had just landed in Tom's back garden. Tom
jumped out of bed, rushed to his window and saw, saw
nothing. He felt very disappointed. He said to himself,
'I must go downstairs to explore.'
He was one of those clumsy, dopey, idiotic boys who read
adventure stories and think they're the hero. (Back to the
story). He put his coat and slippers on, and went downstairs
quietly so not to wake his parents. He went outside and
closed the door behind him. There was mud splatted
everywhere and then he saw an eye. It blinked and Tom
blinked back. He slowly moved forward, tripped over
something and did a head over heels. A dopey voice said,
'Hello, and who may I ask are you?'

The long story

Fortunately in many schools nowadays we have managed to
escape the weekly treadmill of an hour set aside for story-
writing. Most stories my children produce are written over a
period of time which may be as long as a month or six weeks.

Children need a little time for ideas to develop. I try to put
forward the notion of writing a long story at the end of a week
so that ideas can be mulled over at the weekend and discussed
on Monday before the actual writing begins.

Some children will want to map out their stories in advance –
chapter by chapter – so that they have a structure to work to.
Others will prefer, like many authors, to make a start and then
see where the story takes them. This can be quite a time-
consuming activity for teachers, as ideally children should be
able to come and discuss their work at the end of each chapter.
However, with the right organisation where stories are being
worked on at different times of the day, it is possible for time to

be set aside for meaningful and productive dialogue. Apart from talking about the chapter that has just been completed, I always ask if the author knows where he is going next. Sometimes we discuss several possible directions until a decision is reached.

As with professional authors, it is best to stop work before an impasse is reached. If there is a new line of thought, it can be picked up next time and the story continued.

I find that stories which include a journey of some kind work particularly well, although on other occasions I have linked story-writing with current project activities.

When the story is complete, i.e., it has been re-written or typed out over a period of time, it can be presented as a proper book with a card cover back and front.

As mentioned in the section on writing picture books, it is useful to examine 'real books' to discover the details included on their covers. Most will contain something about the author and something about the story.

On the back cover of her book *Tom's Secret Dragon*, Claire writes:

> Tom had a friend, a dragon called Zagon. Zagon was kind and came from Gradon. Gradon was another planet. Gradon used to be a lovely place with kind dragons and other small animals, but it had changed to rocks, desert and bones, and all the dragons were evil except the odd one. With the help of Tom and the other kind dragons, they turn it back to how it used to be, or do they?
> Find out in TOM'S SECRET DRAGON.
>
> *Claire Bayntun, 11 yrs.*

Concentration

The poet Brian Jones in his poem *How to Catch Tiddlers*, writes of the concentration needed to achieve such a goal:

*... There is just the net,
the hand, and now, near an old glance somewhere,
a sleek shape holding its body constant,
firm in the fluid world. Move on. Watch
only the net. You are a hand only,
steering, controlling.*

Suggest that children try to think of situations where they are using their powers of concentration to the fullest extent.

Encourage them to write so that the reader can see what they see and feel what they feel. It is difficult to re-create the intensity of an experience, but by drawing upon the right words and phrases, something of what they felt will be transmitted.

Story poems

There is a great tradition of story poems in the English language. Ballads are still a source of pleasure and many poets and song-writers use the ballad form. Poems such as *The Highwayman* by Alfred Noyes or *Flannan Isle* by Wilfred Wilson Gibson are good for reading aloud in the classroom. Poets such as Michael Rosen, in many of his books, and Alan Ahlberg in *The Mighty Slide* have brought the tradition of story poems up to date. Read Rosen's *Chocolate Cake* from *Quick, Let's Get Out of Here* and suggest that the children think of an incident where they have been in the wrong, then try to tell it in the form of a story poem.

My mum doesn't like my friend

My mum doesn't like my friend,
She says he's too cheeky,
But,
I say, 'He's my friend,' and he is.
He lives next door,
And often pokes his head through our hedge,
Then he says, 'Can I come round to play?'
So I ask my mum
And she says,
'No,
He's too cheeky.'
'Why?' I ask.
'You know why,' my mum says,
And tells me what he does.
'He wrecks the garden,
Batters the hedge
And a million other things.'
Then one day I had a plan
That materialised in my brain.
You see there's a house in front of our house
And a lane at the side.

This means there's a house behind ours.
I thought that I could climb over the wall
Into their garden,
Then my friend could help me up
With a rope
That he found at the quay.
So I wrote my plan down
And made a paper plane.
I threw it over the hedge.
He read it.
Then he got ready.
Next I was climbing the wall.
Suddenly one of the big nails I was standing on broke
And I hit my knee.
Luckily I had my jeans on.
I got on top of the wall
And
I jumped.
I landed silently on their lawn.
Then I saw a rope snaking over the wall.
I darted towards it.
Nearer and nearer I came to the rope.
Even though it was only a few metres from where I'd jumped,
It seemed like miles.
My heart felt as though it was in my throat.
I kept thinking it was going to pop out of my mouth.
At last I came to the rope.
I climbed up into my friend's garden.
My plan had worked.
When it was 12 o'clock
I thought I'd better go home for lunch.
I peeped over the wall.
The people who owned that house were inside.
I climbed over the wall.
And jumped.
Then I walked along to the wall behind my house.
Suddenly I realised that I needed a rope to scale the wall.
The next thing I heard
Was a door being opened
And that door was leading to the garden I was in.
Desperately I tried to scale the wall.
Then,
I slipped.
Next thing I knew
I was in hospital
With a bandage round my head.
One day the people who lived in the house behind ours

Asked me why I was in their garden.
I told them I was sitting on the wall and fell backwards
And I wondered if they believed me.

Aaron Turpin, 10 yrs

Quick ideas

Natural history of a unicorn/phoenix/bookworm/Pooh bear

Take any mythical or invented animal and make up a 'plausible' life history. Who were the parents? Where was your creature born? Were there others like it? What does it eat?

Explanations

Explain carefully how to use a piece of equipment. Take it step by step and try to evolve a balance between assuming that your reader is half familiar with the equipment already, and a complete idiot. Suggestions for equipment could include video, TV, camera, telephone, cassette recorder, computer, wordprocessor.

The dream

The American writer Jack Kerouac used a technique of writing in a number of his novels that became known as 'stream of consciousness'. He tried to write fast, without thinking what he was writing and without revising it! Sometimes this kind of writing can produce some startling imagery. Kerouac would often wake up and immediately start to write down his dreams. Children might be asked to write whatever comes into their heads in a similar way, for a period of ten or fifteen minutes. Often the most reluctant writers can produce some unusual results.

The Dream

Swimming, but how? I'm moving, but how? Tomato sauce ocean with bird-people eyes. Flying around in a lettuce bathtub, four sided octagons, moose-headed flies, chocolate jets, dustbin passengers. Banana ships floating nothingless somethings and time-space egg pies, nothing is here, but something is under it. Human head tigers in sky face jungle,

163

air catches flowers, the air away, nothing can stop me in my
lettuce bathtub. The toad jumps out of its book. The exit is
nearer, further than nearer, faster, more faster, faster, faster,
faster, faster ...

Barry Harvey, 11 yrs

The skull

Beg or borrow a skull from your science department or museum
service. Discuss its possible identity! Some children might care to
compose the story of a skull. Suggested starts include – 'The
skull opened its mouth and said ...' or ' "I will tell you who I
am," said the skull.' Warn against being too gruesome, and
invite clever ideas.

How briefly can something be said?

Take a sentence and discuss it, to see how many words can be
removed before the meaning is no longer clear. Try other
sentences. Now write messages using as few words as possible.

Search out birth announcements in the local papers. Composing
an announcement is a good exercise in economy of language;
the more words you use, the more money you pay.

Now try writing a story using only fifty words.

Reading and writing

Writing about writing

How I write

When I write I find it much easier if we all discuss our ideas and how to go about this certain piece of writing. Then I like to think what I am going to write about and how.

I prefer to write in rough first because I can change things. I wrote this in rough first. When I change things I change them because the lines are too long or the words are boring. I also prefer to write in not a silent room but not a deafening one because I feel more relaxed.

I like to read other people's work because I sometimes learn from them. I get my best ideas from thinking what I want to say, but change the words so they sound right and make sense. I keep writing down lots of ideas and the ones which sound original I keep, and the others I either work on or forget about them.

For a piece of perfect writing I read through it and change all the bad and boring words, if I have any, and then I hope that the teacher will say 'very intelligent work'.

Natalie Burdon, 11 yrs

Writing

Writing is something anyone can do. It's like you are the king or master of a land and you can do anything you want.

I've always liked writing, putting my ideas on paper. I've never found writing a story boring because I like my style, if I didn't I would change it.

It makes my characters come alive in a world of their own, I am able to escape from the real world.

I have got to write in silence or my characters and world just become ink on a page and I don't find magic in them.

Jolie Baker, 12 yrs

The Way I Write

Before I start a piece of writing I find it helps to talk about it first because it sort of makes my mind clear of what I've got to do. Some of my best ideas come from my imagination. If an idea appears in my head I quickly jot it down in my rough book and when I have a series of fairly good ideas I begin to construct a piece of writing. I prefer to work in a noisy room because sometimes the words people use in their speech can help create a realistic atmosphere. I usually write in rough first, because then I can change words that I think are boring or just don't make sense.

Alison Crook, 11 yrs

I like to use a smooth piece of paper.

Richard Waspe, 11 yrs

I like to write because I can see my story, the one I've made up, not a TV series or a book or poem, my story, no one else's. I benefit from writing, it stretches my imagination to limits no TV programme could match. I can be anywhere I want in my imagination, anything, any place. It's my mind and my stories. I love writing. It's great!

Greg Everett, 12 yrs

I get ideas from things out of this world which squeeze out from the back of my head.

Kerry Moyler, 10 yrs

I get ideas when the room is deep in thought. Sometimes looking out of the window helps bring pictures to my mind.

Mark Werren, 11 yrs

Why I write

I write because I can be what or who I'd like to be, and do what I'd like to do.

My writing can express my feelings if I like. I like to have conversations and often fantasy, because I know I can never do all those make believe things. Writing about doing impossible things helps; it satisfies me.

I need quiet to write best, but sometimes the conversation and music around me gives me ideas. I can write nearly anywhere if the particular place has the right feeling.

Anthony Barden, 12 yrs

166

I think discussing helps as well so you can share ideas.

Morgan Lloyd, 11 yrs

Writing

When I start to write a piece of writing I always build on a central idea, I prefer to work in quietness. If the piece of writing has to be good then I'm always concentrating. First of all I jot down the ideas, then I arrange them into the piece of writing. I then start to change words, I change non-interesting words for interesting ones ... I like to read others' work and grasp ideas from it. I look at ideas from all sides to find their best meaning and use.

John Manwaring, 11 yrs

I write because I enjoy making things happen which I know will never happen to me, creating pictures which nobody else can see unless they read my stories.

Jolene Hooper, 11 yrs

I do like writing because instead of talking it's another way of explaining.

Farhan Mughal, 8 yrs

When I start to write a story, poem or description I have an idea and a picture. Then I think if it is going to be enjoyable, then jot the ideas down on rough paper. I like to discuss it with the people sitting next to me.

Stuart Townsend, 11 yrs

I like writing because I get exercise in my fingers!

Shakira Keddo, 8 yrs

Writing about books and authors

About the Author

Anna Budd was 10 when she started the book and was 11 when she finished. She lives in Lynsted with her parents and two brothers. She has written and made other books, one called *Dragon's World*, one called *Castle Krill*, one about books, one with her poems in and this one about the Vikings.

Comments on another child's story:

I think the pictures and the story are very good. I liked the cover.

Stephen Fowler

I like the mounting and the drawings.

Philip Folse

The story is very grown up. It is funny in some places and serious in others. I think it should be aimed at 7 or 8 year olds.

Georgina Hammond

The ending was a bit short.

Ralph Wood

When Rod Campbell Visited

Mr Campbell told us a story about the circus and he drew a tent. Then he drew a ring master and coloured them in. Then he ripped it off and drew another one, and he drew a lady riding a horse and the horse was wearing a saddle and a gold chain, and the lady was standing up on one leg. He did another drawing and he drew a tiger jumping into a ring of fire, and because we liked tigers and lions, he drew both of them. The lion was sitting down while the tiger was jumping. He was jumping through the ring of fire, and the ring master was holding a whip, but he didn't hit any one, only if they were naughty. He drew a clown throwing water at the other clown's face and they looked like they were brothers because they were wearing the same clothes.

Richard Petchey, 7 yrs

When Leila Berg Visited

Leila Berg, an authoress, visited our School. She talked to us about how she discovered her ideas. She has written about forty books on her family, her childhood and about special things which have stuck in her mind.

She told us about a book called Tracy's Story, where the idea had come from her daughter. Leila Berg said she had always wanted to wear false eye lashes and that one day she had found a pair of eyelashes on the bathroom floor. She found a match box and put a label on the front 'Animals Breeding'. She sent the box to her daughter.

The parcel arrived at the theatre where her daughter was rehearsing a play. All the girls crowded round and waited for her to open the surprise box. In there, lay the eyelashes.

Leila Berg also told us about a book called 'A Box for Benny', which was based on a game she used to play when she was little, a box with holes in to throw paper.

While she talked to us, Leila Berg showed us a School photograph of her class. She described some of her worst enemies and friends, and other ideas she had used for writing, by listening to conversations.

Leila Berg finally told us to look closely at the person next to us and then to close our eyes. Afterwards she asked three of us to tell her what they had noticed about their partner, that was strange or unusual. Perhaps she might have another idea for her next story.

Karen Lewis, 10 yrs
Jane Cox, 10 yrs

Review of a group story (by another group in the same class):

The whole story was rushed and happened too quickly. The background information was not very well written and didn't say very much, but the ideas were good. There were not very many illustrations and the illustration in chapter one was a little poor. However, the illustration in chapter four was very well drawn. The names were funny but not realistic. The words and spelling were not bad, although they could have been better. At the very end of the story there was too much action, everything happened at once. The writing was well written but not very neat. The front cover was a good idea but the colouring was poor and a little scribbled. Punctuation was good although a few words didn't make sense.

The story was constructive and well put together, we all understood the story although in some places we were rather muddled. The presentation was good and was set out well. We all liked the story very much, it was amusing and enjoyable.

Books alive!

Books alive!

After school I'll fly away
and save a maiden from the worst
revenge of dragons where they play;
it must be so,
I read it in a book you know.

Then I'll climb the mountains high
and plant my country's flag,
lean on my stick with satisfied sigh;
it must be so,
I read it in a book you know.

I'll sail a raft from here to there
and fight the pirates or crocodiles strong,
I'll swash my buckle without a care;
it must be so,
I read it in a book you know.

And when I've recaptured the moon
from evil alien, green and slimy,
I'll weave a web on a spider's loom;
it must be so,
I read it in a book you know.

At last the prisoners will be free
and all the world will be at peace,
then I'll go home and have some tea;
it must be so,
I read it in a book you know.

Robin Mellor

Desert island books

Wes Magee, Headmaster and poet

Treasure Island by Robert Louis Stevenson
Figgie Hobbin by Charles Causley
The Wolves of Willoughby Chase by Joan Aiken
Rabbiting On by Kit Wright
The Coral Island by R. M. Ballantyne
Season Songs by Ted Hughes
William the Gangster by Richmal Crompton
Salford Road by Gareth Owen

Brother in the Land by Robert Swindells
The Castle of Adventure by Enid Blyton

Comment:
A mixture of old favourites I enjoyed as a child, and more modern stories and poems. I began reading poems for children when I became a teacher, and books by today's poets are now among my all-time favourites.

Peter Highmore, Headmaster

These books I have found very useful and enjoyed myself:

The White Horse Gang by Nina Bawden
The Turbulent Term of Tyke Tiler by Gene Kemp
Run For Your Life by David Line
Charlotte's Webb by E. B. White
Jet, a Gift to the Family by Geoffrey Kilner
The Piemakers by Helen Cresswell
Would You Rather by John Burningham
Smith by Leon Garfield
The Worst Kids in the World by Barbara Robinson
Danny the Champion of the World by Roald Dahl

Trevor Harvey, Lecturer in Education and a former editor of 'Bookquest'

Selecting just ten titles has been a difficult task. Those listed below are my current 'Top Ten' – but in six months time, some will probably disappear from the list and new ones be added. The age range also means that *A Parcel of Patterns* (Jill Paton Walsh) and *Divide and Rule* (Jan Mark) do not feature; and, had I been asked to prepare a list of my favourite authors, then Ivan Southall, Nina Bawden, Penelope Lively and Jan Mark would certainly have been included. What I have attempted below is to provide an indication of my reading preferences – a mixture of established classics alongside more recent favourites (listed in alphabetical order, by author's name).

A Rag, a Bone, a Hank of Hair by Nicholas Fisk
John Diamond by Leon Garfield
Elidor by Alan Garner
The Green Man by Gail E. Haley

Momma's Going to Buy You a Mocking Bird by Jean Little
The Pirates' Mixed-Up Voyage by Margaret Mahy
The Great Gilly Hopkins by Katherine Paterson
The Silver Sword by Ian Serraillier
One Hundred and One Dalmatians by Dodie Smith
Gaffer Samson's Luck by Jill Paton Walsh.

Alix East, 11 years, member of Gallery Young Writers, Rye

Matilda by Roald Dahl
Mallory Towers Omnibus by Enid Blyton
Going Solo by Roald Dahl
Boy by Roald Dahl
Superfudge by Judy Blume
The Shadow Guests by Joan Aiken
The Peppermint Pig by Nina Bawden
Woof by Alan Ahlberg
Ramona Forever by Beverley Cleary
Freaky Friday by Mary Rogers

Robin Mellor, Headmaster and poet

My criterion is that the story is unforgettable after one reading.
In no particular order:

The Iron Man by Ted Hughes
The Just So Stories by Rudyard Kipling
The Mouse and his Child by Russell Hoban
The Short Stories of Oscar Wilde
The Hobbit by J. R. R. Tolkien
Alice in Wonderland by Lewis Carroll
Treasure Island by R. L. Stevenson
Marianne Dreams by Catherine Storr
The Very Hungry Caterpillar by Eric Carle

Brian Moses, writer and former teacher

My top ten classroom read-alouds for the 10 – 12 age range:

The Brothers Lionheart by Astrid Lindgren
The Midnight Fox by Betsy Byars
The Fib and Other Stories by George Layton
The Mustang Machine by Chris Powling
Fireweed by Jill Paton Walsh

Rebecca's World by Terry Nation
The Worst Kids in the World by Barbara Robinson
The House of Sixty Fathers by Meindert Dejong
The Machine Gunners by Robert Westall
Danny the Champion of the World by Roald Dahl

Scribing a legend

Following a period of reading and sharing myths and legends,
this story was made up by second and third year junior school
children at Bentley Heath Primary School in Solihull. I acted as
scribe as the story developed, assisting the children as they
worked on aspects of style.

Bill Cronshaw,
Senior lecturer in Primary Education

NORAK THE DREAM-MAKER

'*In the dark days back near the beginning of time there lived a king
called Ebdor. His kingdom was silent and dreary. The people worked
hard in the fields from morning till night – they never spoke because
there was nothing much to speak about. Each day was like the one
before. Each year followed the same pattern – the earth got warmer
and the crops were planted – they grew during the long days when
the sun shone, and they were harvested when the days began to cool.
As they worked, the people were watched by the Krarg – Ebdor's
army whose job it was to report back anything that was said in the
kingdom. Nearly every day the Krarg reported nothing except the
fact that the work was being done. And this made Ebdor feel
powerful.*

*One day there was born in this kingdom a baby boy called Norak –
his parents loved to listen to his happy gurgling noises, and as he
grew his laughter often filled the air like bird song. The Krarg heard
this too, of course, and they told Ebdor about it but he just said that
Norak's noise would disappear in time – he would soon be like
everyone else.*

*But Norak was not like everyone else. He would stand in the fields,
gazing at the clouds scudding across the sky – he would see pictures*

173

in the huge cloud formations. He begged everyone to stop their work to watch the birds in flight and he dreamed of the day when man himself might fly. At night time he watched the stars in the heavens and noticed the changing phases of the moon. Gradually, even the straight crop rows began to change as Norak discovered the beauty of flowers. And the people would smell the flowers and listen to Norak as he described the dreams he had. And what dreams! Dreams of machines that worked for man – powered by the wind or the rushing streams. Slowly, but surely the land changed and the people had created gardens and forests and they talked constantly of the new ideas that Norak pushed into their minds.

Soon the Krarg had so much to tell the king that he couldn't take any more. 'Bring me that boy!' roared Ebdor. 'My people are becoming lazy!' And with no more ado, he had Norak thrown into the deepest, darkest dungeon in the castle.

A short time later, some travellers came to Ebdor's kingdom. They were trying to cross the dark lands and the way had been dull and dreary. Imagine their delight when they came upon the incredible things in Ebdor's land! Immediately they begged to be taken to see the king. When they were brought to Ebdor they bowed low. 'Majesty', they said, 'far have we travelled but never have we seen such splendours as your kingdom offers. Pray teach us your ways for we will pay you handsomely and your words will enlighten the dark lands.' Ebdor was proud and pleased that they should find his kingdom so interesting. He summoned Norak from the dungeon. 'This is Norak, the dream-maker,' said Ebdor. 'He has shown my people many things.' The travellers listened spellbound to Norak and they returned to their own land, having paid Ebdor, to pass on the message of the dreams.

So Norak became Ebdor's dream-maker and soon everyone in the kingdom learnt how to dream their own dreams and they talked and shared ideas. Ebdor's land prospered and flourished. Gone were the grey, silent days. Norak the dreamer had changed all that. . .'

Writing our own story

Being Alone is an account of how Eirlys felt on her return to school following the death of her father.

Being alone

I feel reclusive, sad and lonely. I sit in the corner of the field or playground and feel depressed. I get lost in thought, cut off from the outside world. Bewildered, distressed and tense I sit there. I feel conspicuous but no one can help. Thinking about the once joyful but now unhappy past, the future seemed just enough to handle. Worried about home, the rest of the day at school and the future. There seems no end to it. Apprehensive to come into the classroom again, to face the teacher, the class.

I walk into the line feeling as conspicuous as anyone ever could. I get on with the day. My feelings start to change. My friends chat. I hear the hub-bub of the class talking. I don't feel alone anymore. My friends come over to me. They comfort me and tell me a good joke.

Suddenly I'm laughing. The world is a good place. I feel relaxed and happy, contented, and nothing feels wrong, sad and depressing anymore.

Eirlys Evans

The journey I will never forget

by *Tran Dang* (aided by *Mrs Averil Weekes*)

I lived in Vietnam and my name is Tran. I am ten years old. I shall try to tell you how I came to leave my country and why it was necessary to do so.

The story begins with my grandfather who was a good doctor but Chinese not Vietnamese. He had plenty of money and bought his food from Chinese shops. He treated his patients well and they paid him, not in money, but in goods or things they could catch, like fish or chickens which they kept.

My father also had some medical knowledge and would help people. There were many injuries through sport or through carelessness. My father was only sixteen. Some people were grateful for what they did but others were envious particularly of the lovely house we lived in, set in a garden with a separate cooking house, separate toilet outside. The house had two large downstairs living rooms, one for our family, which was mother, father, three girls and one brother Tuong. My grandmother died very young but grandfather and my father kept a room of remembrance for them where there was a picture of her.

One day the police came to our house and we were ordered to form two groups in the town square. My sisters already had been bullied at school by older girls. In one group stood the Vietnamese and in the other ourselves, the Vietnam/Chinese, of which there were about twenty to forty people. They asked, would we like to stay in the country as servants and be housed in poor farms and grow crops? We would have to live off the land with no money or we could leave the country completely. Some of the Chinese/Vietnamese were sent immediately to far off farms. The Vietnamese took immediate possession. My father, together with other Chinese and Vietnamese, who did not want to live in a country where there was always fighting, decided to get together, pool their money and buy a boat.

Terrible things were happening all around, Chinese burning down Vietnamese villages and confusion reigned everywhere. We prepared to get on board the boat. All was left behind but the little money we had after buying the boat was hidden all over our clothes, in our hems, cuffs, in collars, under hats and all we carried were pots and pans used for eating rice. The boat lay at anchor not far away and was large, brown and white.

The sea that day looked rough and as we approached ready to board many were crying, men and women. My mother and my two sisters were crying and said that they could not come with us as she was Vietnamese and could not face the stormy sea and leave her home country. I embraced them for the last time and we stood on the deck waving goodbye until they were just little dots. It was very sad.

My father took charge of the organisation on the boat. He knew which men he could trust to help him. Even so there was fighting because, at times, there was not sufficient food. It had been decided that the captain and crew should have special treatment and have the best food, but the rest of the passengers should do with as little as possible. For a week our three had to make do with one cupful of rice each and for drinking, the horrible brown water was served in cups. The mothers with babies were not able to feed them, but the new born baby (and there was only one) survived and was a sturdy baby.

About the third day there was a dreadful shock in store for us. We were hit by a freak wave which whirled the boat round and broke the anchor and flung people to the deck. All were seasick and could not keep to their feet. There was vomit everywhere, even on my skirt. Mothers could not help being sick over their children. The wind and rain beat down on us. Women were praying. Next we struck rocks and a hole appeared in the front of the boat. People were soon in the front of the boat. People stripped off their coats and blankets to soak up the water. That left them nothing to protect themselves against the weather.

This foul weather continued for a day but the boat was saved and stayed afloat. At last we saw the sun. We had been in our cabins sitting on the floor trying to rest for we had no hammocks. In the end, the boat was driven towards a lighthouse manned by a Chinaman. He came down to us and helped us over the rocks and towards the land.

After walking about an hour in the wind and rain over hard rocks we finally came to a building which we entered but which only protected us from the wind. Here we lit a fire made of dried leaves and branches and finally we felt warm. There were Chinese people already there who gave us biscuits, very dry, but we were so hungry we ate them gladly.

Next day, the Chinese who befriended us accompanied us in sunshine back to the boat for they wanted to buy from us watches and coats, which they had not seen for sometime. On the same day two fishermen with a small boat said that they could guide us to Hong Kong, but first they must do some fishing. We gave them money for they promised to return and guide us safely to Hong Kong, but they never returned and we never saw our money again either!

We waited all day for the fishermen to return but, despite our disappointment, we had a lovely surprise, for, in the darkness, we suddenly saw lights! Lights! The lights of a big boat and there were people waving, very happy to have found us, for they were from Hong Kong.

Ropes were secured to the prow of our boat and we were pulled off the rocks. A small launch roared into view and the men scrambled on board and asked us many questions and all the passengers were so pleased to see friendly faces again.

We told them of our adventures and our need for food, especially milk for the baby. Back came the boat and with it milk in a bottle for the baby. Each family was given a small bowl of rice which we ate, rationing ourselves to so much for the two days it took to reach Hong Kong.

Hong! Kong! A city of twinkling lights and friendly people. We were taken first to a big house and interviewed by the Press and the Police. That night we were given some reasonable food and water and we slept on the floor. Regrettably the toilet was dirty just as it had been on the boat.

The Police came the next day with water, cold water in which we were allowed to wash ourselves and our clothes taking only one hour in all, so that our clothes were damp when we put them on.

After three days we went to a different house. We had luckily been picked as one of ten families where there was only the father and no wife. The rest remained and spent another two weeks in the first big house.

We spent a month in Hong Kong in four different houses which were quite clean, but where the cooking was very difficult as we had to share with several families and the kitchen was far from where we slept. My father went out to work and I spent my time cooking or stopping Tuong from fighting all the other boys.

Finally, my father told us that we would be going to England (where it would be raining all day we were told) but this was not true.

Now, after those many adventures, I live happily in England; for my father was wise and did not listen to people who ran down England. He said England would be a good land in which to settle.

At the end of the flight we landed in a cold, wet place but were given a kind welcome by nurses who checked our hair, teeth, throats and then gave us a good meal. Everyone was very happy and friendly and I thought to myself, 'I think we shall like this England ...'

Stories and the national curriculum

English for Ages 5–16 provides the background thinking to the attainment targets and programmes of study for English in the National Curriculum. Quite rightly, it recognises the place and importance of story: 'Narrative has been described as a primary act of mind; children construct the world through story.'

Sharing a response to story-books

The report recognises that:

'Learning to read and learning to write are intimately related. By reading a wide range of literature, children become aware of new forms of discourse and modes of expression with which they may experiment in their own writing.'

'Pupils should be encouraged to respond to all forms of literature in ways which they find pleasurable, and hence which are likely to promote understanding. Their response should be stimulated through a range of active strategies.'

Excerpts from the programmes of study for reading, taken from the Statutory Orders for English in the National Curriculum (March 1990):

Key Stage 1

'Teaching should cover a range of rich and stimulating texts, both fiction and non-fiction, and should ensure that pupils hear stories, told or read aloud ...'

'Reading should include picture books, nursery rhymes, poems, folk-tales, myths, legends and other literature ...'

'Pupils own writing – either independently written, or stories dictated to the teacher or composed in collaboration with other pupils – should form part of the resources for reading.'

'Activities should ensure that pupils:

● hear books, stories and poems read aloud ...

- retell, re-read or dramatise familiar stories and poems;
- make their own books . . .
- talk to the teacher and each other about the books and stories they have been reading or listening to;
- ask and answer questions about what has been heard or read – how characters feel, their motives, the endings of stories.'

Key Stage 2

'The material available must pose a significant challenge to pupils . . . folk-tales and fables might include translations from original sources. Pupils should discuss with others and with the teacher what has been read.'

'Pupils should:

- hear stories, poems and non-fiction read aloud;
- have opportunities to participate in all reading activities, eg preparing and reading a selection of poems, reciting some from memory, or taking part in story-telling sessions or dramatic activities . . .
- keep records of their own reading and comment, in writing or in discussion, on the books which they have read;
- read aloud to the class or teacher and talk about the books they have been reading;
- be encouraged to respond to the plot, character or ideas in stories or poems, and to refer to relevant passages or episodes to support their opinions.'

Pupils working towards level 5 'should be helped to look in a text for clues about characters or actions, and to use these clues to reach conclusions, evaluate and predict what may happen'.

Helping children develop as story-tellers

Both the Cox report and the statutory orders are quite clear in recognising the role of speaking and listening not only in children's development as story-tellers, but also in their development as readers and writers.

Excerpts from the programmes of study for speaking and listening:

Key Stage 1

'The range of activities designed to develop pupils' ability to speak and listen should include:

- listening and responding to stories, rhymes, poems and songs – familiar and unfamiliar. These should include examples from different cultures and authors and from pupils' own work;
- discussion of their work with other pupils and the teacher;
- collaborative planning of activities ...
- talking about experiences in or out of school ...
- telling stories ...
- collaborative and exploratory play;
- imaginative play and improvised drama.'

Key Stages 2 to 4

'Pupils should be given the opportunity to learn how to:

- express and justify feelings, opinions and viewpoints ...
- discuss increasingly complex issues;
- recount events and narrate stories;
- assess and interpret arguments and opinions with increasing precision and discrimination;
- present their ideas, experiences and understanding in a widening range of contexts across the curriculum and with an increasing awareness of audience and purpose;
- listen and respond to an increasing range of fiction ...
- recite and read aloud in a variety of contexts ...

'The range of activities should include:

- the preparation of presentations ...
- talking about stories, poems, playscripts and other texts.'

Children as authors

The report quite clearly bases its approach on the view that young children should be treated as authors.

'Good primary teachers pay attention to the process of writing, developed from knowledge and understanding of the practice of experienced writers (including themselves); they are then able to provide classroom practices which allow children to behave like real writers.'

The links between reading and writing stories is clearly made.

'Young children hear stories either told or read from a very early age and, as soon as they have the skill, they read them themselves. In this way they internalise the elements of story structure – the opening, setting, characters, events and resolution. Similarly, they come to realise that, in satisfying, well-structured stories, things that are lost will be found, problems will be solved, mysteries will be explained, and so on.'

Excerpts from the programmes of study for writing:

Key Stage 1

'Pupils should have frequent opportunities to write in different contexts and for a variety of purposes and audiences, including for themselves.'

'Pupils should see adults writing. Teachers should write alongside pupils, sharing and talking about their writing ...'

'Pupils should be enabled to compose at greater length than they can manage to write down by themselves, by

- dictating to their teacher or another adult, or into a tape-recorder; or

- working with other children; or

- using a word processor ...'

'Pupils should:

- undertake a range of chronological writing including ... stories ...

- play with language, for example by making up jingles, poems, word games, riddles and games ...'

'Pupils should write individually and in groups, sharing their writing with others and discussing what they have written, and should produce finished pieces of work for wider audiences, eg stories ...'

'Pupils should be asked to write in response to a range of well chosen stories, poems, plays ...'

'Pupils should discuss their writing frequently, talking about the varied types and purposes of writing ...'

'Pupils working towards level 3 should be taught to recognise that writing involves:

- decision making – when the context (the specific situation, precise purpose and intended audience) is established;

- planning – when initial thoughts and the framework are recorded and ordered;

- drafting – when initial thoughts are developed, evaluated and reshaped by expansion, addition or amendment to the text.'

Key Stage 2

'Pupils should:

- be helped to increase their control of story form, through their experience of the stories they have read and heard, recognising for example, that the setting and the outcome need to be made explicit to the reader ...'

- have opportunities to create, polish and produce individually or together, by hand or on a word processor, extended written texts, appropriately laid out and illustrated ...

- write in response to a wide range of stimuli, including stories, plays and poems they have read and heard ...

- be encouraged to be adventurous with vocabulary choices ...

- think about ways of making their meaning clear to their intended reader in redrafting their writing.'

Depending on the activities, other parts of the programmes of study may be carried out. The approach and activities outlined in this book will form part of the range of experiences needed to assist children in reaching the various statements of attainment. The more obvious statements that children might be helped to achieve are shown below:

Attainment target 1: Speaking and Listening

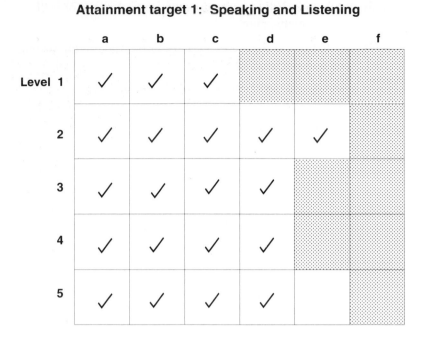

Attainment target 2: Reading

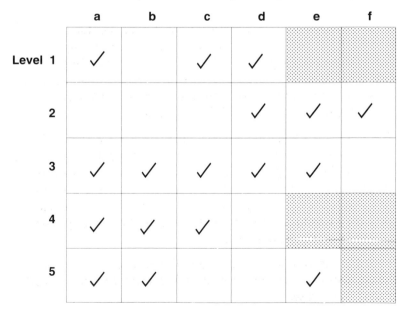

Attainment target 3: Writing

Further books which may prove useful

Teaching Literature Nine to Fourteen by Michael Benton and Geoff Fox (Oxford University Press). Essential purchase for upper juniors and middle schools. Many tried and tested ideas for introducing literature into the classroom. Also an examination of what happens when we read stories and poems, plus extensive lists of recommended reading material.

Did I Hear You Write? by Michael Rosen (André Deutsch). A really accessible read. Rosen examines the child, his culture and his way of speaking, drawing upon vast experience as a poet/ performer in schools. The notion of children writing from their own experience, relating something they want to in the way that they want to, is central to Rosen's thinking. Many starting points for the classroom teacher too.

Poetry in the Making by Ted Hughes (Faber). Still one of the best books about the writing process, with excellent advice on both poetry and prose.

Developing Reading 3–13 and *Children's Writing in the Primary School* by Roger Beard (Hodder & Stoughton). The first book is a compendium of advice about the teaching of reading. There is a particularly useful chapter on 'The Experience of Literature', which includes lists of all the books that won major book awards between 1970–1985. The second book is a survey of the development of writing in schools, with some useful insights into the creative process.

Tell Me Another by Bob Barton (Macmillan Education). Packed with advice on story-telling – selecting a story, learning the plot, bringing the characters to life, story-telling in the classroom, etc.

Developing Response to Fiction by Robert Protherough (Open University Press). How children read fiction at different ages, plus a guide to selecting novels for children. Includes five chapters contributed by classroom teachers, each concerned with a different approach to the class novel. Useful for upper juniors/middle schools.

Working with Fiction by Michael Hayhoe and Stephen Parker (Edward Arnold). Advice on extending children's reading and writing abilities through the enjoyment of fiction. Chapters on talk, drama, visual and written activities. Again, for the older end of the age range.

Creative Writing for Juniors by Barry Maybury (Batsford). First published over twenty years ago, but revised and updated recently. Lots of practical ideas.

Young Words (Macmillan). Award winning entries from the W. H. Smith Young Writers Competition. Published annually. Well worth browsing through each year to see the kind of standard that can be achieved.

The Way to Write by John Fairfax and John Moat; *The Way to Write Novels* by Paddy Kitchen; *The Way to Write for Children* by Joan Aiken (Elm Tree Books). An excellent series of writing manuals for teachers who would like to extend their own writing capabilities.

The Signal Selection of Children's Books edited by Nancy Chambers (Thimble Press). Published annually. A survey of recommendations by teachers, librarians, booksellers, etc.

Telling the Tale edited by Liz Weir (Youth Libraries Group, Remploy, London Rd, Newcastle under Lyme, Staffordshire ST5 1RX). A useful booklet containing a collection of articles on aspects of story-telling.

Storytelling by Eileen Colwell (Bodley Head). A readable, practical guide to the art of story-telling. If you want advice on how to take the first steps into telling tales, you need look no further.

And None of it was Nonsense by Betty Rosen (Mary Glasgow Publications). The story of a talented teacher making use of story-telling as a way of opening new horizons with a multicultural group of boys not too confident about their abilities.

Review magazines:

Books for Keeps edited by Richard Hill. Six issues a year. Details from 1 Effingham Road, Lee, London SE12 8NZ.

Bookquest edited by Brian Moses. Three issues a year. Details from the Literacy Centre, Brighton Polytechnic, Falmer, Brighton BN1 9PH.

Other resources

4 Mation Ed Resources, Linden Lea, Rock Park, Barnstaple, Devon EX32 9AQ. Suppliers of 'Box of Treasures' computer software.

The National Community Folktale Centre publishes a list of story-tellers. Available for £1 from The National Folktale Centre, All Saints, White Hart Lane, London N17 8HR.

Books referred to in the text

Ahlberg, Janet and Alan – *The Jolly Postman* (Heinemann)
Ashley, Bernard – *Break in the Sun* (Puffin)
Bawden, Nina – *Carrie's War* (Puffin)
Billam, Rosemary and Ottie, Vanessa Julian – *Alpaca in the Park* (Picture Lions, Armada Books)

Briggs, Raymond – *The Snowman* (Picture Puffins)
Browne, Anthony – *Gorilla* (Mammoth)
　　　–*Willy the Champ* (Magnet)
Burnett, Frances Hodgson – *The Secret Garden* (editions by
Puffin, Armada and Magnet)
Burningham, John – *Mr Gumpy's Motor Car* (Picture Puffins)
　　　– *Mr Gumpy's Outing* (Picture Puffins)
　　　– *Would You Rather ...* (Picture Puffins, Armada Books)
Byars, Betsy – *The Night Swimmers* (Puffin)
Cooper, Susan – *The Dark is Rising* (Puffin)
Cunliffe, John – *Postman Pat's Safari* (Hippo)
Dahl, Roald – *The BFG* (Puffin)
　　　– *Boy* (Puffin)
　　　– *Danny the Champion of the World* (Puffin)
　　　– *James and the Giant Peach* (Puffin)
　　　– *The Magic Finger* (Puffin)
　　　– *The Witches* (Puffin)
DeJong, Meindert – *The House of Sixty Fathers* (Puffin)
Durrell, Gerald – *My Family and Other Animals* (Penguin)
Fine, Anne – *Bill's New Frock* (Methuen)
Gallaz, Christopher & McEwan, Ian (ed.) – *Rose Blanche* (Cape)
Holm, Anne – *I am David* (Mammoth)
Hughes, Ted – *The Iron Man* (Faber)
Hunter, Mollie – *The Kelpie's Pearls* (Magnet)
Hutchins, Pat – *Goodnight, Owl!* (Picture Puffins)
Jones, Terry – *The Saga of Erik the Viking* (Puffin)
Juster, Norton – *The Phantom Tolbooth* (Armada Lions)
Kafka, Franz – *Metamorphosis* (Penguin)
Kerouac, Jack – *The Book of Dreams* (City Lights Books)
Layton, George – *The Fib and Other Stories* (Armada Lions)
Lee, Laurie – *Cider with Rosie* (Penguin)
Lewis, C. S. – *The Lion, the Witch and the Wardrobe* (Armada
Lion)
　　　– *The Magician's Nephew* (Armada Lion)
Lindgren, Astrid – *The Brothers Lionheart*
　　　– *Pippi Longstocking* (Puffin)
Maddren, Maureen (ed.) – *Free Stuff for Kids* (Exley
Publications)
Magorian, Michelle – *Goodnight Mister Tom* (Puffin)
Maris, Ron – *Are You There, Bear?* (Picture Puffins)
　　　– *I Wish I Could Fly* (Picture Puffins)

Morpurgo, Michael – *Friend or Foe* (Magnet)
Naidoo, Beverley – *Journey to Jo'burg: A South African Story* (Armada Lions)
Nation, Terry – *Rebecca's World* (Beaver)
Needle, Jan – *Albeson and the Germans* (Armada Lions)
Pearce, Philippa – *Tom's Midnight Garden* (Puffin)
Powling, Chris – *The Mustang Machine* (Knight)
Prater, John – *The Gift* (Picture Puffins)
Price, Susan – *The Ghost Drum* (Faber)
Prince, Alison – *How's Business* (Deutsch)
Robinson, Barbara – *The Worst Kids in the World* (Beaver)
Rodgers, Mary – *Freaky Friday*
Sendak, Maurice – *Where the Wild Things Are* (Picture Puffin)
Serraillier, Ian – *The Silver Sword* (Puffin)
Stevenson, James – *The Worst Person in the World* (Picture Puffins)
Storr, Catherine – *Clever Polly and the Stupid Wolf* (Puffin)
Strachan, Ian – *Journey of 1000 Miles* (Magnet)
Swift, Jonathan – *Gulliver's Travels* (Many editions)
Thomas, Ruth – *The Runaways* (Beaver)
Tolkien, J. R. R. – *The Hobbit* (Unwin)
Townsend, Sue – *The Secret Diary of Adrian Mole Aged Thirteen and Three Quarters* (Methuen)
Waddell, Martin – *Can't You Sleep, Little Bear?* (Walker)
Walsh, Jill Paton – *The Dolphin Crossing* (Puffin)
   – *Fireweed* (Puffin)
Westall, Robert – *The Machine-Gunners* (Puffin)
Wicks, Ben – *No Time To Wave Goodbye* (Bloomsbury)
Williams, Jay – *The Practical Princess* (Hippo)

Poetry mentioned in the text:

Browning, Robert – 'The Pied Piper of Hamelin' (Many editions)
Coleridge, Samuel Taylor – 'Kubla Khan' (Many editions)
Gibson, W. W. – 'Flannan Isle'
Jones, Brian – 'How to Catch Tiddlers', from *The Spitfire on the Northern Line* (Chatto & Windus)
Nicholls, Judith – 'Late for School', from *Magic Mirror* (Penguin)

Noyes, Alfred – 'The Highwayman', (Oxford University Press edition) illustrated by Charles Keeping; or from *I Like This Poem* (Puffin)
Poe, Edgar Allan – 'Eldorado' from *I Like This Poem* (Puffin)
Reeves, James – 'The Sea', from *The New Dragon Book of Verse* (Oxford University Press)
Rosen, Michael – 'The Chocolate Cake', from *Quick, Let's Get Out of Here* (Puffin)
Turner, Walter James – 'Romance', from *I Like This Poem* (Puffin)

Acknowledgements

Work by children

Material included in this book was written by children attending the following schools: Lynsted and Norton C.P. School, nr. Sittingbourne; Freda Gardham C.P. School, Rye; Marshlands C.P. School, Hailsham; Tunbury C.P. School, Chatham; King Offa C.J. School, Bexhill; Monkton C.E. Primary School, Thanet; Durrington High School, Hove; Bourne C.P. School, Eastbourne; Pebsham C.P. School, Bexhill; Woodingdean C.P. School, Brighton; Herne C.E. Primary School, nr Herne Bay.
A number of examples of work were produced by members of 'Gallery Young Writers' in Rye, 'Surrey Gifted Young Writers' (S.E. Area) and 'Tunbury School Writers Group' run by Melanie Corbett. 'The Coal Miner' by Nico van der Wurf was first published in the W. H. Smith competition anthology *Young Words* (1985).

Other material appeared in *Bookquest*, the Swale Divisional Anthology; *Words out of our World* (King Offa C.J. School); *The Freda Guardian* (Freda Gardham C.P. School); Marshlands School magazine; and *Poetic Writing in the Primary School* by Pie Corbett, published by the Kent Reading and Language Development Centre.

Thanks to the many children, teachers and writers whose approaches to story we have learnt from, in particular Chris Powling, Chris Eddershaw, Neville Sherman, Jenny Carter.

Thanks to Pam Shepherd of Herne C.E. Primary School for permission to reproduce her children's *Jolly Postman* letters. Thanks also to Robin Mellor, Bill Cronshaw, Wes Magee, Trevor Harvey and Peter Highmore for their contributions. Also Sheila Freeman for inviting me to Croydon to run the Magic Box workshop.

'How to Catch Tiddlers' by Brian Jones from *Spitfire on the Northern Line* published by Chatto & Windus.

'Books Alive' by Robin Mellor appears by kind permission of the author.

'Advice from Jill Paton Walsh' collected from notes made on a Surrey young gifted writers course.

'Advice from Roald Dahl' published in *The Times*, 8 July 1989 as part of a children's short story competition.

'Stories are magical': this phrase has echoed in my mind for years. I am grateful to the original author of this idea, whoever that might be, for where I first read or heard it I cannot recall.

Every effort has been made to contact copyright holders. The authors and publisher would be glad to hear from anyone whose rights have been infringed.

Postscript

'Writing is another common magic,' said the witch, 'and the first step you must take in it is to learn the alphabet of this book, to learn what words these signs are speaking to you from the page. This is the simplest kind of writing-magic, but it is strong and not to be despised! When you can read this book, Chingis, the voice of a witch who has been dead two thousand years will speak to you from it. Every day, people who know nothing more of witchcraft, open books and listen to the talk of the dead. They learn from the dead, and learn to love them, as if they were still alive. That is strong magic.'

From *The Ghost Drum* by Susan Price.